GEN Z CO-AUTHORS

Tina Ahuja
Nathan Bawduniak
DaniAnn Costagliola
Molly DiGregory
Corinne Dougherty
Julia Dwight
Matthew Goetz
Julianne Greco
Matthew Gross
John Hartofilis
Meghan Hom
Zachary Jones
Gregory Kane
Jesse Kay
Gorav Kumar
Anthony Lanza
Charles Lapolla Jr.
Lord Gerald Marapao
Ana Micevska
Sabrina Motiwala
Emma Murphy

Kyle Neville
Kristyn Norkus
Daniel Pennell
Sara Persau
Eloi Pradier
Jesse Priest
Olivia Ryker
Brianne Salera
Sergio Scardigno
Joseph Schneider
Jaisal Shah
Sashank Sindhia
David Smolyak
Rachael Spelman
Marija Stojkoska
Brendan Sullivan
Mark Tenbrink
Jon Valcarce
Jing Wang
Naomi Zheng

Published by Richard Dool

ISBN: 9781089330547

First Edition: August 2019

Manufactured in the United States of America.

DEDICATION

One of the characteristics I love the most about Gen Z is their genuine desire to make a difference—to change the world. Community consciousness is a defining characteristic of this generation.

They've even been called "Philanthroteens."
They're not simply dreaming about making a difference someday in the future.

Jeff Fromm, CMO Network

We are dedicating this book to two very worthy charities.

100% of the net proceeds of this book will be donated equally to:

A GEN Z SNAPSHOT

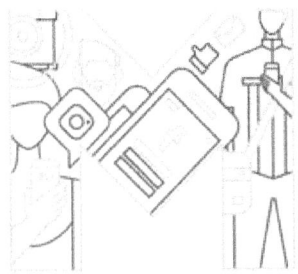

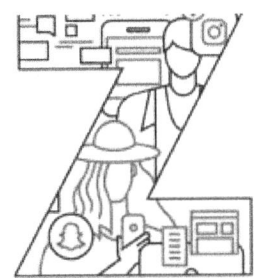

MILLENNIALS

Born between about

1980 & **1996**

MOST WERE RAISED BY
BABY BOOMERS

GREW UP DURING
AN **ECONOMIC BOOM**

TEND TO BE **IDEALISTIC**

FOCUSED ON HAVING
EXPERIENCES

MOBILE **PIONEERS**

PREFER BRANDS THAT
SHARE THEIR VALUES

PREFER **FACEBOOK**
& INSTAGRAM

GENERATION Z

Born between about

1997 & **2010s**

MOST WERE RAISED BY
GEN XERS

GREW UP DURING
A **RECESSION**

TEND TO BE **PRAGMATIC**

FOCUSED ON
SAVING MONEY

MOBILE **NATIVES**

PREFER BRANDS THAT
FEEL AUTHENTIC

PREFER **SNAPCHAT**
& INSTAGRAM

HOW WE CONCEIVED AND CONSTRUCTED THIS BOOK

The idea behind this book came from three intersections. A colleague, Mark Beal, has been writing about Generation Z for some time and his recent book "Decoding Gen Z" prompted my interest to dive deeper into this Generation. I have been immersed with some Gen Zers in my undergraduate classes and I wanted to learn more to create optimal engagement opportunities. Finally, another colleague had an opportunity to interact with a group of Gen Zers in a "Principles of Management" class.

These three intersections promoted the notion of "crowdsourcing" a book on Gen Z to help add to the dialog about this rising generation. It was also a chance for this group of Gen Zers to explore and apply the concepts and practices they were discussing in class.

We explored the literature and thought it would be interesting to gain the Gen Z perspective on want they expect as they enter the workforce—and also how they want to be led. The book was designed to capture the Gen Z voice throughout.

The team of Gen Z co-authors and I brainstormed the book concept, topics and the overall tone and approach. We divided the tasks among Strategy, Editorial, Creative, Technical, Content and Promotion teams.

The team also demonstrated a core value, deciding to donate 100% of the net proceeds of the book to the two named charities.

Overall, it was an ambitious project with a self-imposed timeline of 15 weeks, but the team stepped up and delivered. It was not a completely smooth process, we had some bumps in the process, but stayed focused. "71% of Gen Z say they believe the phrase, "If you want it done right, then do it yourself," and they did.

Dr. Richard Dool

FOREWORD

When I authored *Decoding Gen Z: 101 Lessons Generation Z Will Teach Corporate America, Marketers & Media*, I interviewed Gen Zers across the United States between the ages of 13 and 23 regarding a wide variety of topics including media consumption, social media preferences, marketing, advertising and the workplace. I did not delve deeply into any specific topic, but I offered insights and trends directly from the mouths and minds of Gen Zers across a number of categories that I thought would be of interest to key stakeholders including marketers, media companies and employers.

However, with the publishing of *How Generation Z Wants To Be Led,* Dr. Richard Dool and the Gen Z university students he collaborated with and crowdsourced, offer every employment recruiter, human resources executive, manager, supervisor and senior company executive the essential guide for how to recruit, hire, manage, mentor and lead the next most important cohort at the workplace.

Simply stated, this book should be mandatory and required reading for anyone who plans to recruit, hire, manage, mentor, retain and lead anyone who graduates from college starting in 2019!

In this book, Dr. Dool and his Gen Z co-authors cite a statistic that should be a wake-up call for anyone who manages and leads employees – "by 2020, Generation Z will make up an estimated 30% of the workforce and 40% of the consumer market. Remarkably, 65% of them will work in jobs that don't even exist yet, as technology plays a major role in their lives."

Starting in 2020 and with each passing year, Generation Z will not only comprise a larger percentage of every employer's workforce, but they will deliver greater influence and impact. The brilliance of *How Generation Z Wants To Be Led* is that the book is written from the perspective of Gen Z and offers insights directly from today's university students - your future employees.

Many employers have admitted that they made mistakes as Millennials joined the workforce and became a significant physical and vocal presence. There will be no excuse with Generation Z as this book was written by Gen Zers and offers employers this cohort's perspective and attitudes on critical workplace topics from recruiting and retaining to communication, collaboration and conflict resolution.

Having been raised with technology in their hands from the age of one, Gen Z is the most tech-savvy segment to ever enter the workforce. With that, these digital natives bring to employers an entrepreneurial spirit, team-first attitude, proactive approach and a solutions-oriented mindset. Unlike previous employees, Gen Z is not looking to be hired to simply receive and complete tasks. They want the opportunity to offer solutions to business challenges that will make their workplace more efficient and effective.

Additionally, while Gen Z is being recruited and retained, they are conducting their own analysis and evaluation of potential employers, seeking to be employed by organizations that prioritize inclusion, diversity and even purpose over profits. They are attracted to employers who represent much more than just getting the job done, but serve a greater mission and welcome diverse experiences, background and thinking as part of a more holistic approach to the workforce as a community of learning, exploration and evolution.

Everything Generation Z is looking for in an ideal employer following graduation ultimately ladders up to leadership at all levels in an organization. One excerpt from *How Generation Z Wants To Be Led* summarizes it powerfully in three sentences. "Gen Z Leaders focus on purpose and unity within an organization, and they provide clear shared goals with their colleagues.

They forge creative, innovative visions that express the organization's core values. Gen Z's effective communication skills and fostered collaborative skills provide value to teams."

As you read *How Generation Z Wants To Be Led,* pay close attention to the specific words that come from the minds and mouths of the book's Gen Z co-authors as it relates to what they describe as the most important qualities and characteristics of their ideal future employers – inclusive, diverse, innovative, transformative, collaborative, communicative, community, culture, purpose, mentorship and work-life balance – to highlight just a few.

If you take quality time to listen and learn from Dr. Dool and the Gen Z co-authors of *How Generation Z Wants To Be Led*, you will set yourself, your fellow employees and your company up for success in hiring and retaining Gen Z employees now and for the next 20 years in a way that will transform your organization and deliver measurable business impact across people, purpose and profits.

Mark Beal

TABLE OF CONTENTS

INTRODUCTION

"Gen Z is a very unique generation and I think we are going to make a significant impact on the workforce."

Gen Z Student, Age 19 - Stevens Institute of Technology

Our rationale for writing this book is to offer some insights about Gen Z, primarily focusing on how Gen Z will impact the workforce and their preferences on how to be lead. After careful research, we discovered that there was little information published about how Gen Z wants to be lead. When we identified this gap, we decided that we should fill it by writing and publishing our own book. What further makes this book unique is that it not only fills a gap on this type information—it is researched and written by members of Gen Z.

Our goal in writing this book is to educate more people on Gen Z through this unique lens. We aimed to write the book in a way that would be beneficial for people of all ages to read, and since it is primarily written by members of Gen Z, readers will hopefully have a better understanding of how Gen Z thinks and acts. We hope that members of the Millenial, GenX and Baby Boomer generations will read this to learn more about this new generation currently joining the workforce. They can learn more about how Gen Z thinks and operates and be better prepared to make their arrival into the workforce a smooth transition. We also want members of Gen Z to read this book to learn more about themselves and their future coworkers. They can use this book to make themselves more familiar with the tendencies and behaviors of a typical Gen Z worker, so they can better understand and have stronger relationships with their coworkers once they enter the workforce. We want this book to be valuable to readers of all generations.

This book covers a variety of different topics about Gen Z's view of the workforce. Topics discussed include how members of Gen Z were raised, their journey through life and the events that shaped them, and how they differ from previous generations. We discuss how these attributes and qualities of Gen Z members could impact the ways they will act in the professional world, and we look at specific aspects of the workforce that are particularly unique and important for Gen Z. We discuss topics like workforce expectations, talent management, and motivations. We also cover more practical things, including how Gen Z works in teams, how they deal with conflict, and how they communicate about and deal with change. While this book does cover a wide range of topics about Gen Z and the workforce, it is ultimately a guide to Gen Z, written from the Gen Z perspective. We hope that readers learn something new that they can put into practice in their professional or personal lives.

We would like to thank all of our readers for giving us a chance to share our unique perspectives. We hope this book will provide an overall understanding of how Gen Z will impact the present and future. Since every co-author is a part of Gen Z, we put a lot of effort into our goal of offering the best and most complete perspectives possible. We wanted this book to be something that all past, present, and future generations can read and enjoy, but most importantly learn from. Finally, we hope readers will use that knowledge to better contribute to the workforce and even in their daily lives.

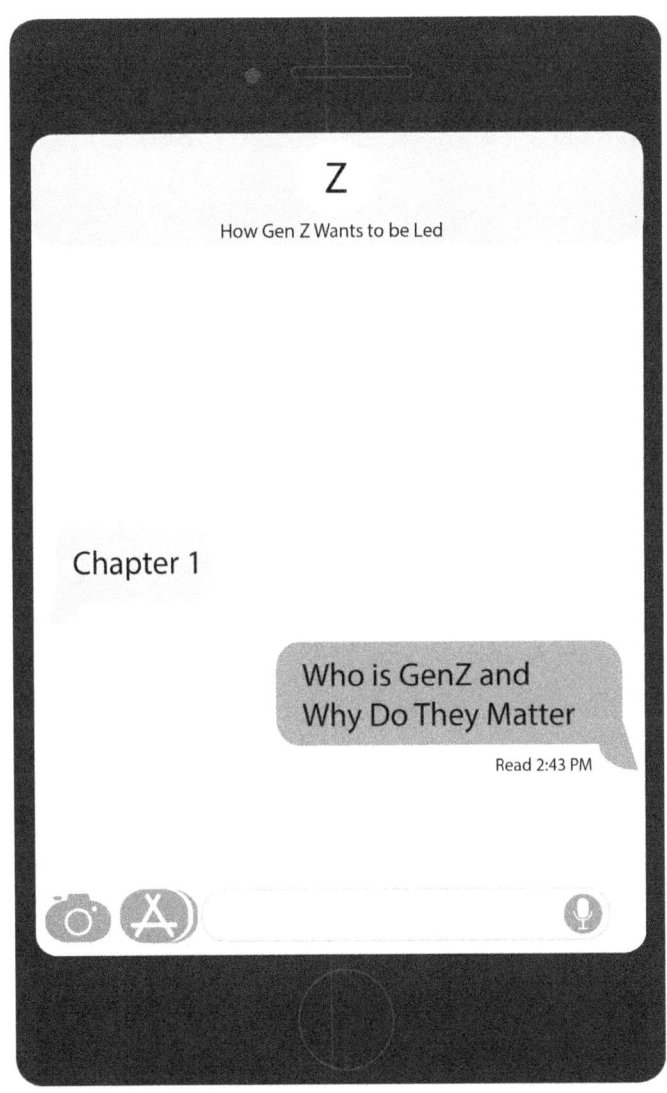

Z

How Gen Z Wants to be Led

Chapter 1

Who is GenZ and Why Do They Matter

Read 2:43 PM

"I think that our generation will have a huge impact on the workforce. Our use of technology and the way we were raised really set us apart from other generations."

Gen Z Student, Age 19 - Stevens Institute of Technology

(Moring, 2017)

Who is Generation Z? Most researchers agree that the older members of Gen Z were born between the mid-1990s and the early 2000s (Williams, 2015). There are some differing opinions on how to precisely define the age range of Gen Z, but this is currently difficult to evaluate because generational researchers typically need to wait for the generation in question to grow up before they can determine a specific cutoff (Dimock, 2019). The general consensus is that the oldest members of Gen Z are in their early to mid-twenties as of 2019, which means they have graduated college and recently entered the workforce (Dimock, 2019). Gen Z will have a significant impact on demographics in the United States, and will be the most ethnically diverse and largest generation ever (Fry & Parker, 2018). Subsequently, this will have major impacts on the demographics of the workforce, which is why there is an urgent need to understand and prepare for Gen Z.

Every generation is shaped by several different factors, including their parents' generation, the cultural and social trends that defined their upbringing, and major events that occured in their lifetimes, both domestically and globally. For example, even the oldest members of Gen Z are too young to have fully experienced 9/11, but they are certainly aware of the impact it had in the United States and around the world. Specifically, members of Gen Z grew up in a constant state of war and intervention in the Middle East, and the oldest members of Gen Z have been aware of the conflicts therein for their entire lives. Gen Z were also raised under the Patriot Act, and witnessed the revelations made about mass surveillance by government agencies like the NSA. To members of Gen Z, a lack of privacy is not alarming, it is just a reality of the world they live in. This makes Gen Z more acutely aware of privacy and internet security risks than previous generations. Gen Z is also painfully aware of the 2008 financial crisis, as many Gen Z kids were affected by their parents' monetary and career downturns during the crisis and in the years following. After feeling the effects of the crisis firsthand, Gen Z kids know how devastating an economic downturn can be, and many know that they need to prepare for whatever is on the horizon.

The cost of higher education has risen significantly in the United States over Gen Z's lifespan, leaving many members of Gen Z with the choice of either committing to staggering levels of student debt or considering alternatives to higher education. These events certainly shape Gen Z to have an interesting outlook on life; Gen Z saw the harsh realities of the world their parents live in, which gives them a more "realistic" outlook. Gen Z realizes that the world is full of difficult times, and that they need to be prepared for the kinds of events they grew up around. Members of Gen Z make decisions about work and education with financial security in mind, rather than dreams or aspirations, which may not promise the same financial security.

"I'm passionate about music and for my entire childhood I wanted to be a musician, but I chose to study engineering in college because of the financial security. I wish I could follow my dream, but as I grew up I realized that was somewhat unrealistic, and I know I can continue music as a hobby."

Gen Z Student, Age 20 - Stevens Institute of Technology

Not all events that shaped Gen Z have been negative. Many events in the United States and around the world have positively influenced Gen Z. Consider Barack Obama's election and Presidency; while other generations perceived the first African-American president as a tremendous accomplishment, it was simply a reality for Gen Z. Gen Z has a perception of the world that is more diverse and more inclusive, which demonstrates the broader idea that Gen Z is generally more open-minded when it comes to cultural issues, including same-sex marriage, gender identification and race relations (Parker, Graf & Igielnik, 2019).

"The majority of the people I know are more accepting of those issues than the older generations. I think that's because we are exposed to more due to social media."

Gen Z Student, Age 19 – Stevens Institute of Technology

Members of Gen Z have seen Millennials break barriers to enter careers that have been traditionally associated with a particular gender or race, and they are more accepting of women and minorities being voted into public office than other generations (Parker et al., 2019). These are all important and positive facts that define Gen Z; they are more accepting and understanding, which is ultimately beneficial to a changing workforce.

"I think Gen Z is synonymous with Technology. It's a part of every single thing we do."

Gen Z Student, Age 18 - Stevens Institute of Technology

As the first generation to grow up with modern technology already around them, members of Gen Z were inherently familiar with it, instead of having to adopt it the way earlier generations did. Because it was a part of their lives from day one, Gen Z has a much stronger understanding of the ways technology works. For example, it is seen as totally normal for Gen Z kids to be playing on their parents' iPads or other technological devices in public settings like a restaurant or a supermarket—a departure from prior generations.

Like prior generations, it was common for Gen Z kids to grow up playing video games instead of playing sports or doing other activities, but it has also become standard for Gen Z to receive smartphones at an earlier age; only the oldest members of Gen Z remember a time when modern smartphones weren't ubiquitous. Communicating on cell phones and other messaging apps for essentially as long as they can remember, members of Gen Z possess adept skills that are beneficial to the workforce.

Because Gen Z has communicated via technology for their entire lives, they are innately effective, efficient and comfortable with electronic communication—an essential skill in the modern workforce. They are also more aware of what goes on around the world, thanks to the immediate access to a plethora of different ideas and viewpoints that 24/7 news and constant connectivity provide.

Events in the United States and around the world, disseminated through technology, have shaped Gen Z into what they are today: the largest and most diverse generation to date, skeptical but still realistic about how to succeed in the world. This understanding of what life has to offer, along with an emphasis on inclusivity and tech fluency makes Gen Z a truly unique group with a lot to offer the workforce.

For Gen Z, technology played a much greater role in the process of searching for colleges compared to previous generations. The internet made everything easier, from selecting an institution to identifying a major of study. Students can not only search for information about colleges and majors, but also other important factors like financial aid, teacher reviews, and job-success rates.

"I think the reason is that I want to get better education, and also grow my network with others, so I can be prepared for my future career development. The way I prepared for college was that I got to know what I expected and know how to achieve that goal."

Gen Z Student, Age 22 - Stevens Institute of Technology

One of the biggest factors when searching for colleges is figuring out how to pay for it—both before and after graduating. Of course while there is tuition, and room and board, many students also have to worry about the types of loans earlier generations (includingmany of their parents) are still paying off. According to a study by the National Association of Realtors, Generation X has the highest average student loan balance: around $30,000 (Josuweit, 2018). To alleviate this issue, Gen Z students are finding new ways to save money. While searching for colleges, Gen Z students are increasingly using online services to attain additional scholarships through different means (for example, making a video, writing an essay, or sometimes even signing up for sweepstakes).

Like prior generations, many Gen Z students in high school and college take retail and service industry jobs to build up savings, but many others are considering starting up their own businesses. According to a Gallup Student Poll, 40% of students in grades 5-12 plan to start their own business, while 24% are already learning how to start and run a business (Zimmerman, 2017).

"I expected to learn something. I honestly didn't learn very much and my professors were much less helpful than I expected from an expensive school."

Gen Z Student, Age 19 – Stevens Institute of Technology

Upon their arriving at college, students have to adjust to an entirely new life experience and prepare for what is ahead during their four years of being an undergraduate. Like every generation, Gen Z comes to college for an academic experience that will help them grow and prepare for their future career. Students expect an authentic learning experience from a professors who deeply cares about their education. Gen Z wants professors who not only know the material, but teach with enthusiasm and help students better understand the content. They also expect professors to be willing to meet with them to help them with any questions necessary. These expectations of a professor are needed so students and parents alike can make the tuition worth it.

In the last decade, Gen Z has been using technology (laptops, smart phones, and tablets) not only for social media and entertainment, but as a reliable educational tool. While some members of older generations may view such technology as purely time wasters, Gen Z students are well aware of the useful advantages these devices can provide in a learning environment. For instance, when a group of students needs to study for an upcoming test it is very common to use an application such as Google Docs to create a peer-to-peer study guide.

"[Technology has] definitely made it a lot easier. I can access lecture notes at any time and if I miss a slide in class, it's no problem. Furthermore, I can collaborate on projects without ever having to meet up with people, which was especially helpful

in high school because most of my group members lived in a different town than me"

Gen Z Student, Age 20 - Stevens Institute of Technology

Technology is not only useful for studying or facilitating group projects, but also for minor research on education itself, from actual college searches to reviews about professors. This can help students find classes that are right for them and even help colleges improve in certain ways. Gen Z students also expect professors and staff members to be efficient in their use of technology. Like the workforce, technology is always changing and every staff member must find ways to adjust and keep up.

At college, Gen Z is looking for ways to show their interests and expand themselves. Common activities outside the classroom include student organizations, clubs, or sports. Because the college environment is very diverse, students will often share their creativity and opinions within the more comfortable environments of these organizations or clubs. Participating in extracurricular activities can help Gen Z students improve their interpersonal skills and their network. They also benefit from learning about new activities and topics not covered in the classroom. Most importantly, extracurriculars help students find a sense of talent and belonging.

"I do graphic design and music production along with my friends at Fordham. Through these hobbies and running a record label, I have met some of my best friends for life. I've grown so much through the hardships of music publication, promotion, and deadlines for art. I've become better at graphic design and have a deeper appreciation for music. I have a special bond with my friends I share these hobbies with as if they were my family through them, I've learned to be a better, more confident person as we worked together. Overall, I've improved tremendously."

Gen Z Student, Age 19 - Fordham University

"I would say I'm preparing for my career just by balancing all my schoolwork with my personal responsibilities, I guess- not only that, I also try to keep learning outside of class so I can be prepared for situations I might face in a workplace"

Gen Z Student, Age 20 - Stevens Institute of Technology

Preparing for an internship, cooperative education program, or professional employment is similar to preparing for college. Of course, every college has resources and materials to prepare students for their future, but then there are online alternatives like LinkedIn and Handshake, which can help students identify job and internship opportunities. These resources also give specific requirements, so students can find an opportunity that is best suited and most realistic for them. Students have the opportunity to network with students from classes and extra-curriculars, and even upperclassmen and alumni can help offer guidance.

As more and more members of Gen Z start to join the workforce, professional environments have begun to drastically change. Gen Z professionals have introduced and implemented changes ranging from technology-based enhancements to diversifying staff, and even changing perceptions around work-life balance. The effects of this generation have only begun to be noticed in today's workforce because only the earliest portion of Gen Z has yet come of age.

Currently, it is estimated that only 5-10% of Gen Z are active participants in the workforce, but as an increasing number of persons approach the end of their schooling, the workforce has already begun enacting drastic changes in order to attract and lead these individuals (Desjardins, 2019). One of the biggest changes brought on by this generation is the centralization of technology in all aspects of work life. As of 2018, it was found that most Gen Z members spend an average of ten hours a day on the internet or interacting with technology (Desjardins, 2019).

What does this mean for office life? Instead of face-to-face interactions, post-Millenials prefer to communicate on work related topics through email and text messaging. This presents a huge change in day-to-day interactions, and is seemingly unsettling for older generations who thrive in a work environment where human interaction is key to accomplishing short- and long-term company goals. Another major change brought on by Gen Z is the refinement of individual goals. Gen Z members no longer want to work at one company (or two or three) during their professional careers; instead, they are experience-focused and have less aversion to changing professional roles. As a result, companies are continually hiring new employees, which means a lot more money is being poured into the recruitment of new members, as well as benefits to attract individuals to choose a particular company over others.

Additionally, another major aspect of Gen Z's professional aspirations are to acquire leadership positions fairly early on in their careers. Although a lot of upper management positions now have a lifespan of three to five years at a specific company, post-Millennials "seek these positions as a chance to incorporate their ideas and change into the core of a business's funda-mentals." (*Gen Z Student, Age 20 - Stevens Institute of Technolo-gy*).

Not only do these individuals aim to acquire leadership posi-tions, they also seek positions that offer an evolving and chang-ing job focus. Moreover, positions that have constantly chang-ing projects are especially appealing, because Gen Z members get to offer their creative problem solving to a variety of prob-lem areas and can attain extensive experience, which they cov-et. Gen Z's life experiences affect the types of jobs they seek and what's most important to them. They highly value success, with professional and academic achievement ranking as most important. This is further exemplified by the more advanced collegiate degrees that they attain in order to land manage-ment level positions (for example, technology-based degrees as well as the increase in master's degrees attained immediately after students complete their undergraduate degree).

Another way in which members of Gen Z develop and differen-tiate their educational and professional experience from other generations is by focusing their energy on gaining experience. 'Experience' can be obtained through extra-curricular involve-ment while in school, internship opportunities in the field in which students are looking to work, or even company-orga-nized seminars or workshops to learn and enhance one's pro-fessional skill set.

> *"These opportunities are essential to Generation Z members because the notion that their efforts will eventually pay off."*

> Gen Z Student, Age 19 - Stevens Institute of Technology

Gen Z individuals are so dedicated to personal success that they will take lower pay and work long hours on risky projects to gain experience and eventually advance upwards in their professional positioning. Not only is prospective experience necessary to attract and inspire Gen Z members to push themselves, these individuals are also extremely influenced by social issues and many will ultimately work only for companies that have similar interests and beliefs as them. Brands and their interactions on social platforms are becoming such a prevalent factor for individuals when accepting job offers that studies show 77% of Gen Z workers claim a company's diversity and lifestyle would be a deciding factor (Desjardins, 2019).

The most strikingly contemporary change that Gen Z has brought to the workforce currently are their notions on money. Gen Z members are not only willing to put in long hours and hard work, they are also 75% more inclined to relocate to another state for a job offer and 58% more willing to work on weekends (Desjardins, 2019). This most likely is derived from the fact that, upon entering the labor market, 78% have completed an internship or apprenticeship, 35% have started their own business or are in the process of starting one, or that 77% earn extra money on top of their primary jobs through freelance work (Desjardins, 2019).

Not only is this generation extremely hardworking and dedicated, some studies suggest that they may also be more frugal and fiscally responsible than previous generations. For example, 72% say that cost is most important factor when making a purchase, 47% use their phones while shopping to check prices and ask family or friends for advice, and 66% attended college in-state specifically to save on tuition (Desjardins, 2019). Thus, their focus on monetary goals and saving can be used to incentivize and enforce Gen Z individuals to work at peak performance.

Michael Wood, a principal at 747 Insights, told *Business Insider* he's heard Gen Z called "Millennials on steroids," because the generation tends to exhibit similar opinions and beliefs to the one before it—just *more*.

Gen Z - It's the most diverse and inclusive generation yet.
(Kane, 2017)

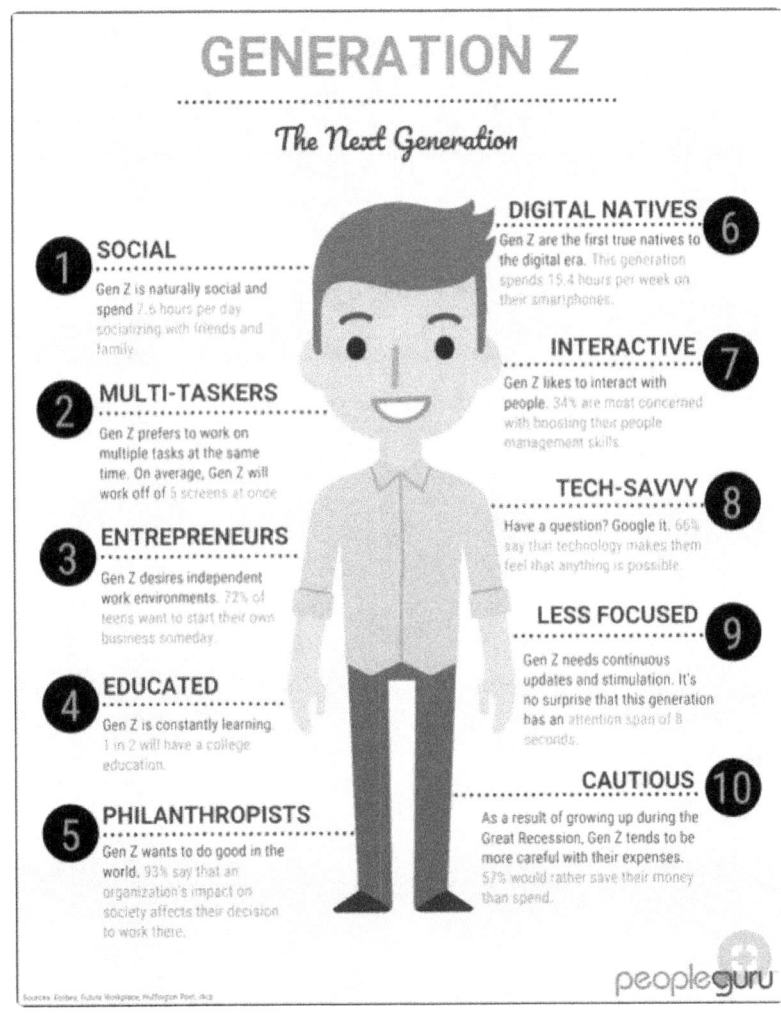

http://blog.peopleguru.com/hubfs/Infographics/Gen%20z.png?t=1537971375329

Characteristics, Values, Beliefs

Baby Boomers	Gen X	Millennial/Gen Y	Gen Z
Optimistic, equal rights, intense work ethic	Skeptical, fun, informal, pragmatic, adaptable, independent, resilient, self-reliant	Realism, confidence, achievement, diversity, collaborative, attention seekers, multi-taskers	Tech savvy, globally connected, flexible, tolerant of diverse cultures
Education is a birthright	Education is a way to achieve success	Education is expensive, enjoy continuous learning	Education is not worth it, success without it through experience
Loyalty is not changing jobs	Loyalty to manager, changing jobs is necessary	Changing jobs is a normal practice	Still undefined on loyalty, but potentially more loyal than Gen Y
No work/life balance	Need balance now	All about work/life balance and flexibility	Doesn't expect work/life balance
Motivated by wealth, rank, prestige	Grew up in uncertainty and turmoil; leery of authority	Grew up with scheduled childhood; trusting of authority	Want to impact the world – high value on social responsibility
Good team players, service oriented	Least likely to be difficult to work with, cynical or condescending	Shaped by the Internet and WWW – instant access to information	Still learning about this generation – more to come.

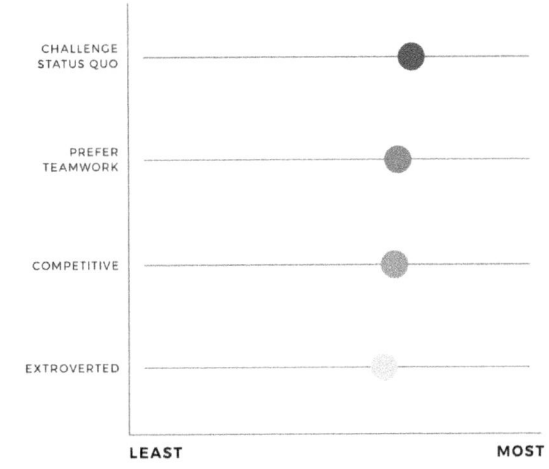

GEN Z PERSONALITY
OVERALL

CHALLENGE STATUS QUO

PREFER TEAMWORK

COMPETITIVE

EXTROVERTED

LEAST   MOST

https://ripplematch.com/journal/article/a-comprehensive-look-at-what-generation-z-wants-in-the-workplace-fa8o8aco/

CHAPTER REFERENCES

Desjardins, Jeff. "Meet Generation Z: The Newest Member to the Workforce." Visual Capitalist, 12 Mar. 2019, www.visualcapitalist.com/meet-generation-z-the-newest-member-to-the-workforce/.

Dimock, M. (2019). *Defining generations: Where Millennials end and Generation Z begins.* Pew Research Center. Retrieved From https://www.pewresearch.org/fact-tank/2019/01/17/where-millennials-end-and-generation-z-begins/

Dimock, M. (2019). *Defining generations: Where Millennials end and Generation Z begins.* Pew Research Center. Retrieved From https://www.pewsocialtrends.org/2018/11/15/early-benchmarks-show-post-millennials-on-track-to-be-most-diverse-best-educated-generation-yet/

Fry, R. and Parker, K. (2018). *'Post-Millennial' Generation On Track To Be Most Diverse, Best-Educated.* Pew Research Center's Social & Demographic Trends Project. Retrieved From https://www.pewsocialtrends.org/2019/01/17/generation-z-looks-a-lot-like-millennials-on-key-social-and-political-issues/

Josuweit, Andrew. (2018). *5 Reasons Generation Z Will Be 'Generation Smart' About College.* Forbes. Retrieved from https://www.forbes.com/sites/andrewjosuweit/2018/03/21/5-reasons-generation-z-will-be-genera-tion-smart-about-college/#cc0aebd7888c

Kane, L. (2017). Meet Generation Z, the 'millennials on steroids' who could lead the charge for change in the US. Retrieved May 5, 2019 from https://www.businessinsider.com/generation-z-profile-2017-9

Moring, M. (2017). Catching Some Z's. Retrieved May 5, 2019 from https://factsandtrends.net/2017/09/29/Gen Z-single-page/

Williams, A. (2015). Move Over, Millennials, Here Comes Generation Z. Nytimes.com. Retrieved From https://www.nytimes.com/2015/09/20/fashion/move-over-millennials-here-comes-generation-z.html

Zimmerman, Kaytie. (2017). Make Way of Gen Z Entrepreneurs Saying No To College. Forbes. Retrieved from https://www.forbes.com/sites/kaytiezimmerman/2017/12/17/make-way-for-generation-z-entrepreneurs-saying-no-to-college/#3ded31d147a6

GEN Z AUTHORS

KYLE NEVILLE
Kyle is a freshman at Stevens Institute of Technology and he is majoring in Accounting and Analytics. Kyle is interested and engaged in this research because he believes it will help him understand his future coworkers and help him understand his value in the workforce.

LORD GERALD MARAPAO
Lord Gerald is a freshman at Stevens Institute of Technology and is majoring in Business and Technology (concentrations include Marketing, and Arts & Technology). He is devoted to helping older generations understand Generation Z as a whole and even learn more about his own generation as well.

RACHAEL SPELMAN
Rachael is a sophomore at Stevens Institute of Technology and is majoring in Business and Technology with concentrations in Marketing and Information Systems. She is interested in this topic because she wants to get her master's degree in Project Management and wanted to learn more about how she can positively affect the workforce once she enters.

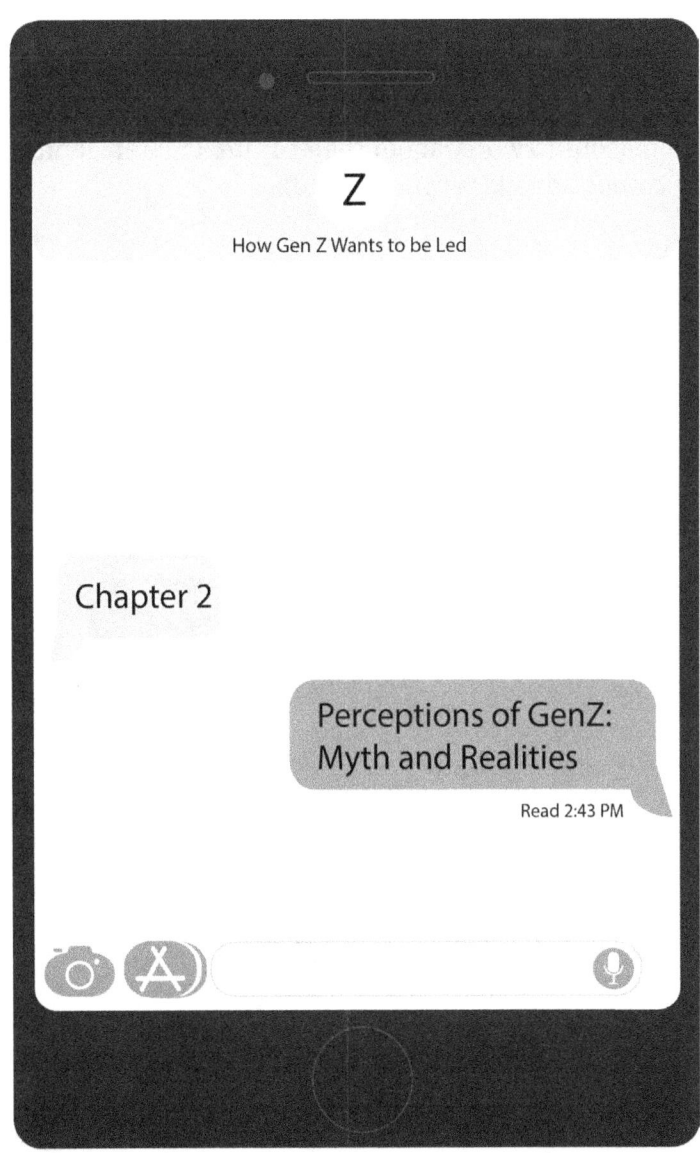

Z

How Gen Z Wants to be Led

Chapter 2

Perceptions of GenZ:
Myth and Realities

Read 2:43 PM

"They Are Not Worried"

Though they are self-learners, 64% of Gen Z say they are concerned about being able to get a job. Members of Gen Z seek mentorship systems to help forge strong skills. They have a lot of reasons to worry about their future. They are living in an age of competitiveness (Bhide, 2016).

U.S. population by generation

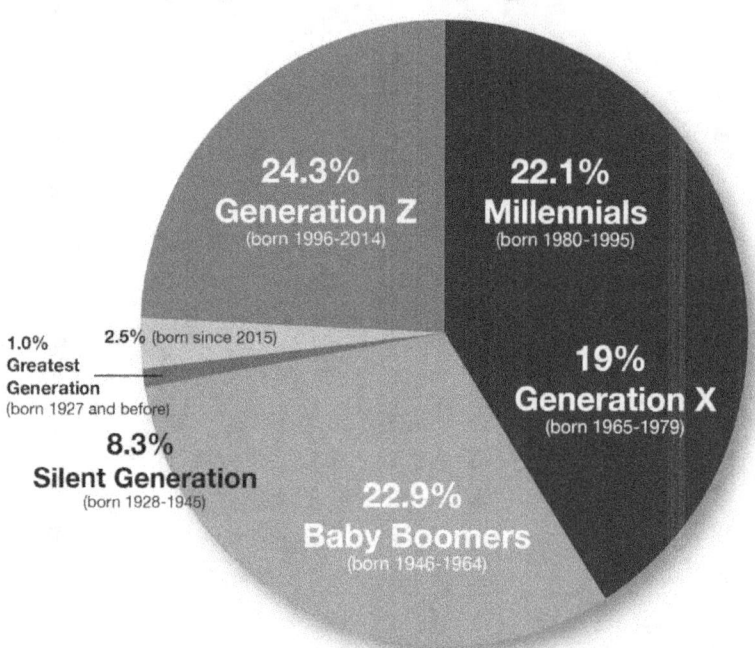

Source: U.S. Census estimates for 2016

Gen Z—those born between 1996 and 2014—makes up 24.3 percent of the U.S. population, according to U.S. Census estimates for 2016, more than Millennials (22.1 percent), Gen X (19 percent), or Baby Boomers (22.9 percent). By 2020, *The Washington Post* suggests Gen Z will have about $3 trillion in purchasing power (Moring, 2017).

They're 60 million people large, don't remember a time before social media, and were raised in the shadow of an economic downturn. And if they're not in your workforce now, they will be very soon. By 2020, Gen Z will make up an estimated 30% of the workforce and 40% of the consumer market. Remarkably, 65% of them will end up working in jobs that don't even exist yet (ITA Group, 2019).

As an influx of Gen Z employees enters the workforce, it is important to clarify any misconceptions or stereotypes. From excessive phone usage to poor work quality and a lack of communication skills, there are many myths to address that mitigate the title of modern day "digital natives," those who have grown up alongside the internet. In reality, Gen Z possess advanced technological skills, and many excel in team environments. Gen Z brings a fresh subset of ethics and skills, and it is important to understand the corporate value that they can provide.

Gen Z is the generation that will soon make up the majority of newcomers in many organizations and businesses. Because Gen Z is going to play key roles in the future and the way businesses and organizations run, their distinct qualities should be understood more. However, this new influx of labor is often misjudged, both for better and for worse. Many people often judge Gen Z as a group who is too busy on their cell phones to do much work. Furthermore, many people also believe that they prefer digital communication over face-to-face interaction, diluting their abilities to communicate effectively.

Ina, Age 19, from Rutgers University, said:

> *"Most people and even teachers have this misconception that when I'm on my phone I am fooling around, scrolling on social media, or texting my friends. But what they don't realize is that the phone is not just a tool for entertainment. It can serve as a tool to get your tasks done. For instance, it is easy to take quick*

notes in class or plan out your schedule. With all the
new functions a cell phone offers, instead of being a
deterrent for productive work, it can in actuality make
work more easily accessible and efficient."

The older generations often disregard the importance of cell phones because of the stigma against it. They believe that everyone glued to their phones must be less focused on reality. In actuality, cell phones loom very large in a young person's life. There are now countless apps that are beneficial in the workplace if utilized properly. Therefore, instead of viewing not only Gen Z, but also cell phones in a negative light, employers should utilize the technology available and Gen Z's knowledge of it for their benefit.

Another common myth about Gen Z is that their communication skills are hampered by their prevalent usage of social media and the internet.

Ivy, from the University of Waterloo, age 18, mentioned:

"People often assume that the increase of technology
is harming our ability to interact with others and
communicate. However, that is far from the truth.
What people do not realize is that technology serves as
another source of communication. One that is equally as
important as face-to-face communication."

Gen Z prefers face-to-face communication over technology: Gen Z grew up with technology, yet 53% percent prefer in-person communication over tools like instant messaging and video conferencing (Millennial Branding, 2014).

The assumption that technology harms one's ability to communicate is viable; however, like Ivy mentions, technology has also become a powerful source of communication because it allows one to access various platforms through the usage of social media and other apps. In the workplace, there are a number of types of communication that need to be mastered in order to be an effective leader, and among them are the various e-forms. When it comes to mastering this source of communication, Gen Z provides one of the best resources because they grew up with it. In addition, even though Gen Z uses technology to communicate more, it does not necessarily mean they lack social skills. When asked if technology hampered their communication abilities, Mina from NJIT, age 20, mentioned that:

> *"No. In fact, technology strengths my communication. When people think of communication through the usage of technology, they often assume texting, but that is not always the case. Not only can I text my friends, I can Facetime them, too. This has, in fact, allowed me to become more sociable because I'm so used to face-to-face interactions."*

Contrary to the assumption that younger workers want "constant connection" via technology, a majority of Gen Z respondents say they prefer in-person communications with managers (51%), as opposed to emailing (16%) or instant messaging (11%) (Millennial Branding, 2014).

When thinking of using technology as a form of communication, it seems to be often forgotten that texting is not the only way that people can interact with each other. There are different apps that allow one to have a face-to-face interaction with others, such as Facetime, as Mina mentioned. Furthermore, technology can also an effective way for people to become more comfortable speaking to a larger crowd. Platforms and apps such as Instagram and YouTube allow one to hold live recordings in which people can interact with colleagues, customers, or other stakeholders. Even though the person in the live recording does not physically see his or her followers, the feeling of people watching his or her every move is still prevalent through constant feedback on live comment feeds.

Joyce, from New York University, Age 20, said:

> *"Social media actually helped me with my stage fright.
> Before I started to make live recordings for my following
> and friends, I would always be very nervous to present
> myself in front of others and speak my mind. But with
> more and more experience with live recordings, I have
> been able to shake off this nerve. Now, when I present
> in front of a crowd, I feel confident. I know what it's like
> to speak in front of hundreds of people, and even if they
> are not physically present with me, the feeling was still
> the same. I still felt hundreds of eyes on me and soon I
> got used it."*

Many people may think that face-to-face communication skills in Gen Z have dwindled because of the increase in technology, but Joyce and Mina highlight that technology can actually be a tool, if utilized properly, to help people overcome discomfort with face-to-face conversations.

The notion that Gen Z is too young to make a difference is often thought of as well. There is a common belief that with age comes experience, but what people do not realize is that the experience of the young is also extremely valuable. Most people believe that Gen Z focuses too much on their phones and technology and are less aware of the real world around them. They believe that Gen Z lives off the stimulated world of virtual reality, which is far from the truth.

The 2014 report by Millennial Branding and Randstad found that 17% of Gen Z want to be entrepreneurs and hire employees. This percent is 6% higher than with Millennials. The increase in desire to start their own business just highlights how Gen Z do not live in a simulated reality. In fact, they have big goals and want to make their mark in the business world.

Stephanie, from Cornell, Age 18, said:

> *"In my prior internships, I have always been given lower trivial tasks that I did not apply for. Even when I became more accustomed to the work environment, I was never handed a task that would allow me to become beneficial to the company and actually feel as though I was a part of it. I feel that one of the main reasons is because of the stigma that surrounds our younger generation. Employers look down on us for our age and especially for the common notion that all we know how to do is fiddle with our phones, but that is far from the truth. I know if I was given a chance, I would be able to prove myself."*

There is often this notion that Gen Z is not prepared for the workforce because of the numerous technology and distractions that surround them. It is not that Gen Z are too involved with a virtual reality that clouds their perception of reality, but rather they are often still not given the chance to reveal their full capabilities and ideas.

Another myth about Gen Z is that many people believe they care more about passion than a paycheck. In reality, it is the opposite that is true. Younger generations, including Gen Z care more about paychecks than their own passions. This favoring of paycheck over passion is caused by the fact that many in Gen Z base their decisions around how it would influence the lifestyle that they want. For example, Gen Z prioritize a more flexible working environment that allows them to work from home, as well as nontraditional working hours.

Tina, from the University of California, Davis, Age 20, stated:

> *"I want a practical life. This is why I chose to major in nursing. It is a safe and stable job for the future that also can guarantee high pay, depending on the hospital and position one is given."*

The notion that Gen Z is unpractical is not true, as many including Tina realize that a paycheck is vital for survival. Even though pursuing one's passions may seem like the ideal lifestyle, the convenience and supportability that a job offers is equally as attractive to many Gen Zers. When asked what they look for in a job, many reply with similar answers—a paycheck, location of job, and time flexibility—that all emphasize the importance of having a job that allows them to live a comfortable lifestyle of their choice. Many companies have also acknowledged this aspect about Gen Z, and have offered more favorable terms for them in order to attract more applicants. For example, the furniture retailer IKEA offers four months of paid parental leave to both full-time and part-time workers with at least one year of experience within the company

For Gen Z, it's not just about the money, for now: Only 28% of Gen Z said money would motivate them to work harder and stay with their employer longer, as opposed to 42% of Millennials. Both Gen Z (65%) and Millennials (69%) say the people whom they work with would enable their best work. While work location is more important to Millennials (47%) over Gen Z (36%), Gen Z (38%) has greater interest in personalizing their own work space than Millennials (34%) (Millennial Branding, 2014).

Ultimately, one of the major misunderstandings of Gen Z is how it is a homogneous group of people. People regard Gen Z as a generation too addicted to their cellphones, lacking communication skills, and too young to make a change. Many times, when categorizing and labeling a group of people, people tend to forget that not everyone's the same. There will always be those who work hard and those who don't, some who care more about money over passion, some who do not, and so on. The differences within a group of people will be never ending because Gen Z consists of a variety of individuals with different mindsets and goals in life. Therefore, instead of labeling Gen Z as a singular group, employers should start seeing and targeting them as individuals who have different talents that can be utilized. They should recognize Gen Z's full potential and strong points of using technology instead of focusing on the negatives.

With these many misconceptions of the Gen Z workers come many realities that show how they can thrive in the workplace. While most employers have been focusing their time on Millennials, it is time for them to focus on the next wave of employees as well. One of the obvious upsides to hiring Gen Z workers is that they are generally accessible 24/7. Instead of working nine-to-five, hours for Gen Z workers can be more flexible. Moreover, with the advancement of technology, employees can now work from home, reducing the need for costly centralized headquarters. Gen Z was born in the digital age, making it easy for them to work in this era. It is said that by 2021, Gen Z will account for 40 percent of all consumers, already outnumbering Baby Boomers and Millennials. This means that their large population will account for a large portion of the workforce and will therefore bring their knowledge of technology and social media skills to the office. They are comfortable with ubiquitous connectivity, highly curated global information, on-demand video, and 24/7 news cycles. In fact, most of them do not even remember a time when social media did not exist. Knowing how to properly manage a social media account for a company is extremely rare and many employers are investing in that skillset. Gen Z are arguably the best for the job.

Gen Z and Millennials both prefer a corporate office space as their top work environment; but Millennials (45%) show a higher preference for a traditional office than Gen Z (28%). Notably, the generations' second choice of work location is a co-working space that operates independently of the employer (Gen Z 27%, Millennials 26%), and Gen Z shows a slight preference for a home office (Gen Z 19%, Millennials 13%) (Millennial Branding, 2014).

"I would say that for the most part every person in Generation Z knows their way around technology, which gives us an advantage over others because we don't have to be trained at our workplace, and therefore they save time and money on hiring us."

Gen Z Student, Age 18 - Stevens Institute of Technology

Most people focus on the technology aspect of Gen Z; however, they are much more than just tech savvy. Training has evolved immensely from past generations. With more knowledge comes more skills and techniques to be learned, and Gen Z are eager to learn. They understand that with the more skills they attain they more desirable they are for employers and the larger paycheck they will receive. They have recognized the importance of training and more and more each day, they are provided with it. According to the Bruce Tulgan (2015), "Soft skills may be harder to define and measure than hard skills, but they are just as critical. People get hired because of their hard skills but get fired because of their soft skills."

It has also been said that Gen Z may be the most educated generation. High school students are taking more college-level courses. College enrollment rates have skyrocketed over the years, becoming so normalized that people don't see another option but to go and finish their education and in many cases pursue advanced degrees.

"I think that our generation strives to be the best, which is why we have such a higher level of education compared to other generations because we hold ourselves to a higher standard."

Gen Z Student, Age 19 - Stevens Institute of Technology

According to the U.S. Census Bureau, higher education attainment of the population has climbed from 24 percent in 1986 to 37 percent in 2014. Gen Z may be a more educated group than ever before, with more than 50% likely to gain a college degree.

GEN Z SEE HIGHER EDUCATION AS THE KEY TO SUCCESS.

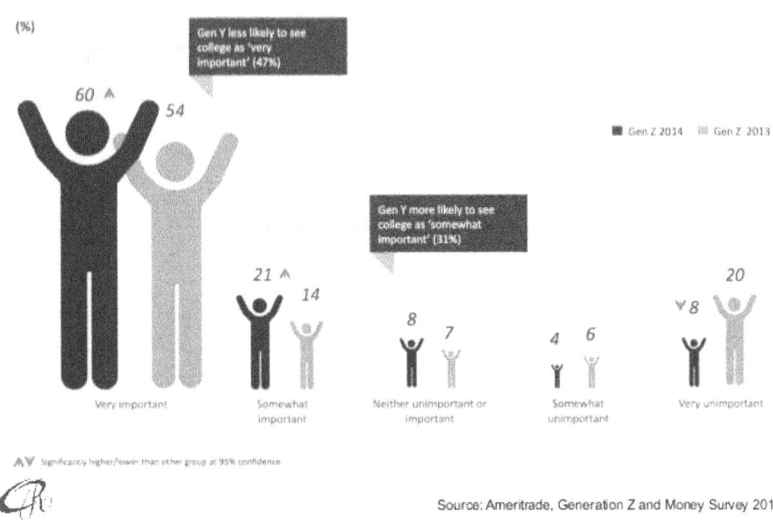

Source: Ameritrade, Generation Z and Money Survey 2014.

Previous generations were traditionally more fearful of change. They were much more conservative. Change meant the possibility of losing their jobs or having to adapt to a new way of doing things. Gen Z's point of view is different because they embrace change and look forward to it. Change is at the forefront of every industry, mostly due to technology. Companies need to change and constantly improve or else they will be left behind. This means they are looking for employees that can see their vision, innovate with them, and travel with them on their journey. Change is a constant in today's world, so it's especially important to have team members who are willing to take on evolving job descriptions amongst other things. Gen Z is all about being more flexible and adapting to the needs of their environments.

Generation Z will be less frustrated in that they're not far removed from their formal education and are still in rapid learning mode.

(Knowledge Path, 2019).

A part of change is diversity: different people, cultures, and ideas to expand a company's reach. Gen Z is the most diverse generation ever. According to NPR, 48% of post-Millennials who are currently between the ages of 6 and 2 are from communities of color. A "bare majority," the report notes, are non-Hispanic white, compared to 61 percent of Millennials in 2002. The world is changing, and so are the people in it.

Gen Z is a multi-ethnic, gender-fluid generation with some key traits that differentiate them from Millennials. Gen Z has grown up in an era defined by the immediacy and extreme connectedness of social media. They embrace diversity and expect brands and companies to do the same (Fromm, n.d.).

Mediakix (n.d.) noted:
> America's Gen Z is expected to be very diverse, as over 50.2% of children will identify as mixed race or as part of an ethnic group in 2020. The "minority white" population will comprise 49.7% of the population in contrast to 24.6% for Hispanics, 13.1% for blacks, 7.9% for Asians, and 3.8% for multiracial populations. Overall, Gen Z is optimistic about diversity in regards to gender, race, and sexuality.

Competition is the root of change in the workplace. Companies change their prices to compete with other companies, they change their marketing scheme to compete with others for a certain demographic. Competition is everywhere. Gen Z appears to be much more competitive with their colleagues than previous generations, focused on a do-it-yourself mentality at work. They want to work on their own and be judged on their own merits rather than those of their team. Competitiveness has been ingrained in the minds of Gen Z since a very young age. Gen Z understands that there's a need for constant skill development in order to stay relevant.

"We're looking to compete a little bit more, we've got a little bit more self-drive, and that also kind of falls into some of the events and conditions that shaped my generation," writes Jonah Stillman, the 19-year-old author of "Gen Z @ Work: How the Next Generation is Transforming the Workplace."

"We [grew up] in the midst of the recession. We saw the downfall of the economy. We saw our parents struggle so much at home," Stillman continues. "So, as we enter the workforce, money is very, very important to us."

This shows that Gen Z has had this competitive edge shown to them at a very young age through the struggles of their parents. There's a greater emphasis on being successful, especially in the workplace and when it comes to making money.

"Watching my parents struggle has given me the advantage I have today, because it has taught me to work hard and compete at the highest levels in order to be successful."

Gen Z Student, Age 18 - Stevens Institute of Technology

Gen Z is willing to work hard, but they expect to be rewarded for it. Increasingly competitive educational standards have driven children to strive for the best grades in their classes. Gen Z thrives in this environment. With the increasing requirements to get into college, Gen Z has become the most competitive generation yet in regard to schooling, which is very important to employers. Employers have also increased their standards when hiring employees. For any company to achieve longevity, they must be both competitive and able to adapt. Gen Z embodies both of these principles.

In the corporate world, where leaders spend 80% of their time communicating, knowing how to use technology is a necessity. While some of Gen Z may appear young and inexperienced to older generations, they provide a fresh lens and perspective and are equipped with technological experience. They have adaptability, and they take on a different approach as leaders. Gen Z enjoys passionate work and an organizational culture that pushes self-growth. Many focus on self-improvement, and they care about motivation in forms other than a paycheck; they value security. With this mindset comes increased competition.

Gen Z leaders focus on purpose and unity within an organization, and they provide clear shared goals with their colleagues. They forge creative, innovative visions that express the organization's core values. Gen Z's effective communication skills and fostered collaborative skills provide value to teams.

"I look for coworkers who respect me despite our generational differences."

Gen Z Student, Age 19 - Montclair State University

With emphases on respect, enthusiasm, and trust, Gen Z creates strong interpersonal relationships. Along with their effective communication, many leaders focus on verbal praise instead of a negative reward system. Gen Z takes challenges and problems head on and they are not afraid of accountability.

"I want to make an impact, gain connections, and immerse myself in the culture of my workplace."

Gen Z Student, Age 18 - Rutgers University

Gen Z workers are effective communicators. They know how to utilize technology to stay up to date with the latest news and changes in the world and in touch with one another.

"In such a fast-paced world, it's hard to find time to meet up with friends and family in person. It's impossible to balance a work life, a social life, and getting an education without the assistance of technology."

Gen Z Student, Age 19, - Montclair University

As managers, members of Gen Z cooperate, communicate, and coordinate effective teams with efficiency in mind. While other generations may value independence, teams typically outperform individuals when there are multiple skills, judgement, and experience on the line. Also, teams increase job satisfaction, morale, and enhance employee involvement.

"Teamwork creates more engagement and optimizes tasks, and it's been intertwined within the school curriculum."

Gen Z Student, Age 19 - Montclair University

Gen Z knows that leadership does not rest in any one person, and they are not afraid to involve employees in decision making and to genuinely listen and see them eye to eye. Gen Z is entering a 52% non-engaged, 18% disengaged, and only 29%

engaged workforce, with 71% of employees lacking passion and a deep connection to their company (Class Notes, Principles of Management, March 26, 2019). Modern day managers focus on increasing employee engagement through teamwork and motivation. They also appeal to quality of life changes like including employees in decision making processes and incorporating off-site work locations.

With 76% of the workforce feeling dissatisfied at times with the lack of recognition received for doing a good job at work, Gen Z managers can motivate employees through verbal praise and incorporating systems that positively reward workers, rather than systems that punish workers and promote sheepish behavior in regards to accountability. The top two motivators at work besides verbal praise are completing challenging tasks and maintaining team spirit. Gen Z values motivation as a tool to combat the high cost of employee turnover, further helping their organizations maintain a competitive edge and to spread happiness from employees to clients. While money is a strong incentive, Gen Z also sees beyond it, and they look to improve and refine skills as individuals with focus on security and interpersonal growth. Monetary incentives are not valued as heavily as praise and recognition, but overall work environments are filled with more motivated employees.

Growing up alongside the internet as "digital natives," Gen Z is strongly influenced by reputation and advertising. As a result, shifts in organizational trends have moved towards organization design, leadership, culture, engagement, learning, designed thinking, and workforce management. Work environments have inevitably changed to accustom these new, generational values and skills. More people are now working off-site, with an emphasis on teleworking and mobility. With a demographic upheaval of newer generations with more diverse backgrounds, coupled with modern technology, focus on optimized speeds, and quality employer and worker relations, Gen Z brings positive change and fresh skills to the workforce.

Gen Z is often misunderstood as the generation addicted to their phones and the generation that communicates ineffectively. They are also seen as inexperienced due to being so young, and there is a general notion that they are unpractical. However, these myths are undermined by the ethics and skills that Gen Z possess. Gen Z values a comfortable lifestyle that ties together work flexibility, location, and the paycheck. They have a technological understanding that makes them desirable employers, and they are familiar with positive, effective communication.

Both Gen Z (65%) and Millennials (69%) say the people with whom they work with would enable their best work (Millennial Branding, 2014).

While Gen Z is effective in team environments, they want to be seen as individuals by their employers, as they truly care about passion and self-growth in their careers. Gen Z is constantly in connection with the world due to smartphones and the internet, a good trait for leaders, who spend 80% of their time communicating. Gen Z are effective communicators who want to inspire and motivate others through their honest communication and hard endeavors.

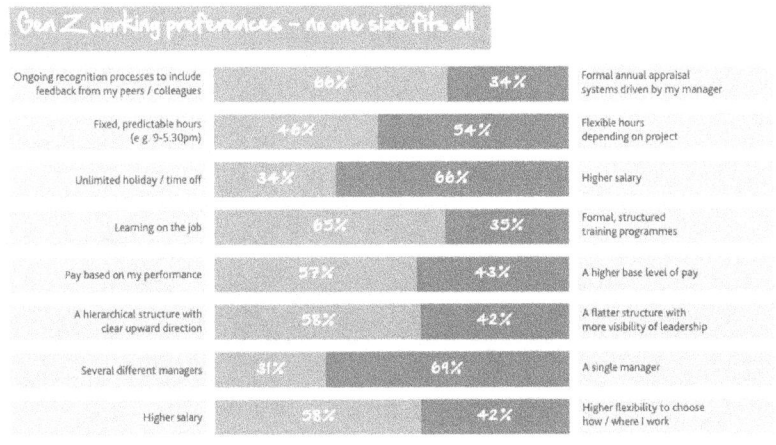

https://www.capita.com/media/2198/generation-z-whitepaper-digital.pdf

Post-Millennials are more likely to be enrolled in college than older generations

Among 18- to 20-year-olds who are no longer in high school, % enrolled in college

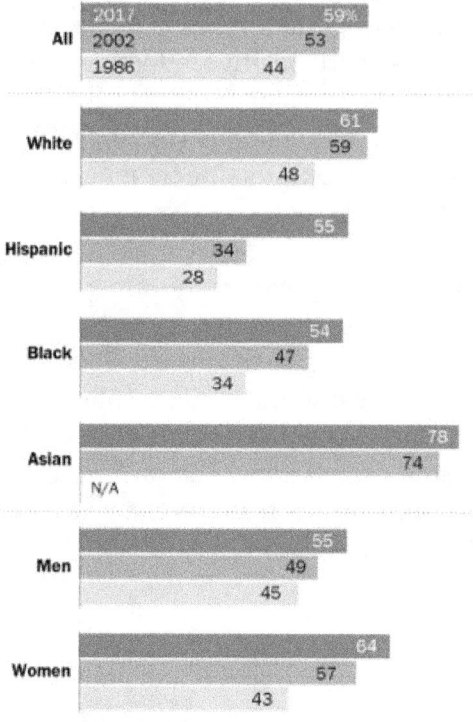

All	2017	59%
	2002	53
	1986	44
White		61
		59
		48
Hispanic		55
		34
		28
Black		54
		47
		34
Asian		78
		74
	N/A	
Men		55
		49
		45
Women		64
		57
		43

https://www.pewsocialtrends.org/2018/11/15/early-benchmarks-show-post-millennials-on-track-to-be-most-diverse-best-educated-generation-yet/

CHAPTER REFERENCES

Bhide, V. (2016). Training Gen Z: 5 Myths Busted. Retrieved May 5, 2019 from https://elearningindustry.com/training-gen-z-5-myths-busted.

Fromm, J. (n.d.) Gen Z Believes Their Generation Can Change the World. Retrieved May 5, 2019 from http://www.millennialmarketing.com/2017/01/gen-z-believes-their-generation-can-ita change-the-world/

Ita group (n.d.) Engaging Generation Z Employees in a Diverse Workplace. Retrieved May 5, 2019 from https://www.itagroup.com/insights/engaging-generation-z-employees-diverse-workplace

Knowledge Path (2019), Generation Z and Change.Retrieved May 5, 2019 from: https://knowledgepathinc.com/generation-z-and-change/

Mediakix (n.d.). The 11 Generation Z Statistics Advertisers Must Know. Retrieved May 5, 2019 from: http://mediakix.com/2017/03/the-generation-z-statistics-you-should-know/#gs.9z0iio

Millennial Branding (2014). Gen Y and Gen Z Global Workplace Expectations Study. Retrieved May 5, 2019 from http://millennialbranding.com/tag/gen-z/

Moring, M. (2017). Catching Some Z's. Retrieved May 5, 2019 from https://factsandtrends.net/2017/09/29/Gen Z-single-page/

Tulgan, B. (2015). Bridging the Soft Skills Gap. How to Teach the Missing Basics to Today's Young Talent. Hoboken, NJ: Jossey-Bass, Wiley.

GEN Z AUTHORS

ZACHARY JONES

Zachary is a freshman at Stevens Institute of Technology and is majoring in Business and Technology with a concentration in Information Systems. Zachary is a part of Generation Z and feels it is important to represent Generation Z instilled idealities that further enhance the desirability of Generation Z employees.

JON VALCARCE

Jon is a freshman Business and Technology major with a concentration in marketing and information systems. Jon is also a men's soccer player at Stevens Institute of Technology and aspires to be a helpful coworker on a marketing team.

NAOMI ZHENG

Naomi is a freshman at Stevens Institute of Technology majoring in Finance. Naomi is a member of Generation Z that represents those interested in becoming a part of the financial and business work field. She believes that understanding Generation Z better will benefit businesses.

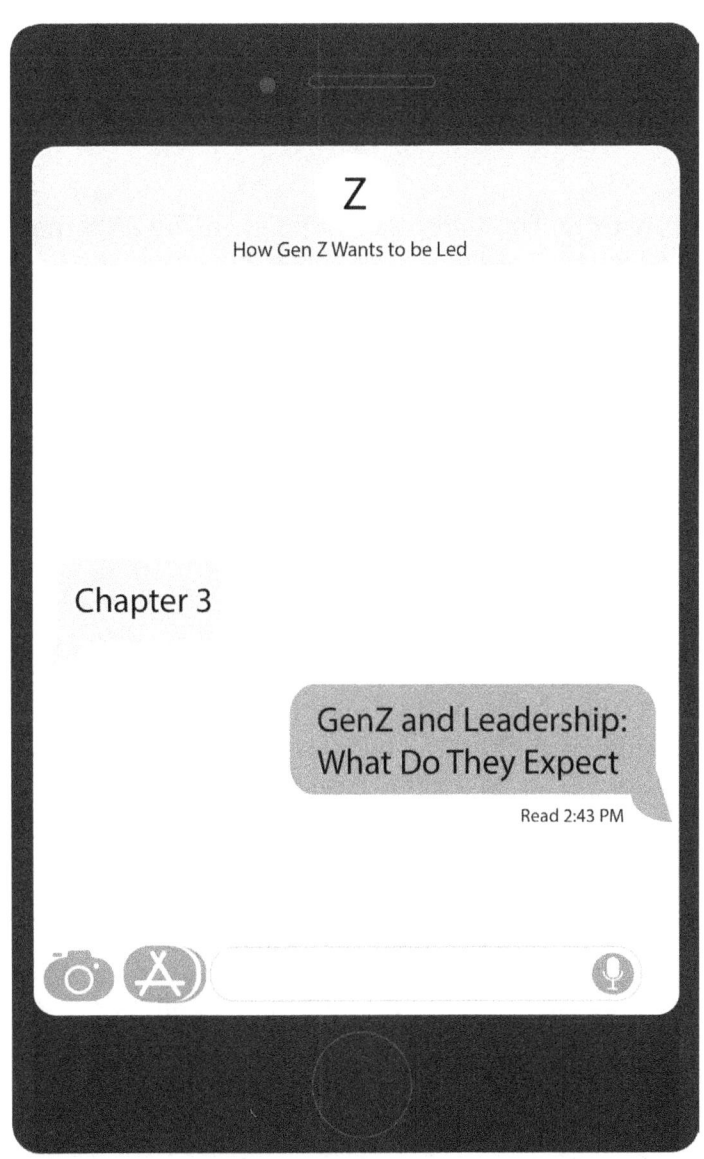

Z

How Gen Z Wants to be Led

Chapter 3

GenZ and Leadership:
What Do They Expect

Read 2:43 PM

83% [of Gen Z] state they expect to make employment changes early on until they find the "sweet spot" where they can achieve their goals. Companies will lose good talent if they cannot provide that "sweet spot."
(Scott, 2018)

There are 69 million Gen Zers in school, and by 2025 they'll be one- fifth of the U.S labor force (Roujol, 2017). Many Gen Zers are not going to want to work a traditional nine-to-five job and possibly relocate for work, either. Today, Gen Zs are not concerned solely about their pay, they care about their purpose in the office, the value of their work, and about incentives and even the amount of paid time off they get. It is important for the new workforce to be prepared for change and to understand what to expect in these upcoming years. Many companies may need to embrace a reality in which nine-to-five is no longer going to be the regular workday and that their cultures are going to have to be altered to meet the expectations of Gen Z.

For Gen Z, one-third (34%) are most motivated by opportunities for advancement, followed by more money (27%) and meaningful work (23%) (Millennial Branding, 2014).

Gen Z grew up with a very different mindset from Millennials and older generations. The growing presence of technology has evolved the way this new generation thinks. Gen Z does not know a world in which a smartphone device is out of hand's reach. They spend an average of 3 hours and 38 minutes on their smartphones, which is 50 minutes more than the average internet user. Growing up surrounded by technology is both a pro and a con when they enter the workforce. While it creates a more independent and competitive environment for Gen Z to thrive in, it also allows for them to be more skilled and flexible in some areas and creates a new form of demand in the workforce.

Gen Z are more likely to pursue a career in technology, being exposed and surrounded by tech so early on in their lives, and research has shown that automation and the proliferation of technology are reducing the need for human intervention in many basic, routine tasks on which entry level professionals once focused. Today, many companies and organizations have asked their entry-level workers to work with data, perform research, and program advanced technologies, while many Millennials that joined the workforce have struggled to move away from entry-level jobs, according to a study by Deloitte (2017). In many cases, a college degree is the basic requirement to qualify for a job, with some jobs even requiring specific prior experience. These shifts in work and expectations, along with economic recessions and advanced technologies, seem to have already begun to have a significant impact on workers.

Although Gen Z workers are far ahead of the curve in terms of adapting and growing in technological skills, some believe they lack in social skills compared to Millennials and any of the older generations. Bruce Tulgan the CEO and founder of RainmakerThinking, a company that has been studying young people in the workplace for 25 years, suggests that Gen Z are only concerned with screen time, and not face to face interaction.

"On the one hand, today's young people are not as comfortable or good at interpersonal communication, of course largely due to growing up communicating on hand-held supercomputers," Tulgan says. "On the other hand, the human element—particularly, supportive leadership and relationships with co-workers—is what matters most to them" (Colletta, 2018).

Deloitte adds that technology has impacted the development of cognitive skills, including intellectual curiosity, among the next generation, creating the risk of skill gaps when they enter the workforce. A shortfall in highly cognitive social skills, such as problem solving, critical thinking, and communication may be an issue. However, most of Gen Z acknowledges the importance of in-person communication and its own deficiencies in this area. Furthermore, in our questionnaire for the students who will be in the Gen Z workforce, 13 out of 15 students responded that they are open to the "do it yourself" attitude, while the two other college students thought that group work is more valuable. This data supports the difference in attitude that Gen Z has from Millennials.

Millennials have been labeled as "entitled" for demanding more flexibility or "flaky" for quickly moving from company to company. One study suggested that 44 percent of Gen Z employees expect to stay with their company around 1-2 years and 37 percent envisioned that they would stay with their company about 3-4 years. In addition, according to a Deloitte study (2017), Gen Z values employment that allows them to live a balanced lifestyle even more than Millennials do. They placed a greater emphasis on physical, mental and social well-being. They want flexibility and control within their schedules. Many Gen Z workers will seek out flexible work hours, progressive benefit plans, and the ability to work from home when possible.

Another one of the questions in our questionnaire was whether current college students preferred to work in offices or at home in the future. 10 out of 15 students stated that they want to work in an office. Unsurprisingly, the top companies that are attracting Gen Z are large tech firms including IBM, Google, Microsoft, Salesforce, and Facebook. The most common reviews on those jobs by Gen Z workers were "work environment" and "flexible hours." Thus, Gen Z is coming into the workforce with high expectations and a very different attitude from Millennials and all the prior generations.

"Independent, Flexible, Impatient"

Gen Z is said to be embodied by the above words when considering the differences between their generation and those before. Members of the Gen Z population describe themselves in this way not in spite nor pride, but out of realization of the type of generation they will be. The workforce is about to experience an influx of workers that have had a childhood unlike any that came before. Reliance on social media, technology, and education in each of these fields sets Gen Z apart from their predecessors in the job market. We took this concept of a new style in the workforce and reached out to Gen Z asking specifically what they believe will "be two distinct differences in work ethic from their parents or grandparents' generations."

We found that Gen Z believes their devotion to technology and reliance on social media will help and hurt them in the workforce compared to earlier generations. Members of Gen Z have a distinct advantage when it comes to understanding technology. Not only have they been able to live through the technological revolution, but thanks to their early exposure they are better able to understand any future advancements in the field. Unlike the previous generations, Gen Z believes that this will give them a competitive advantage of being more "innovative" and "flexible." Their adaptability is a tool they believe will open many doors that the older generations will not be exposed to. Similarly, Gen Z recognized that this also morphs their work ethic into a different style than their predecessors. The new technology will make them more independent, leading to a reworking of the style with which they lead. They see themselves as being much more collaborative and wish to break the stereotype of a lazy, technology-dependent generation.

Similar to the desire to break the negative stereotypes about Gen Z and their ability to lead, the members of the up and coming generation recognize their setbacks. Some believe their generation will have a large group of impatient workers due to a reliance on instant gratification. They are aware that they grew up in a world in which whatever they desired was at their fingertips, ready to be overnighted with one click. However, they have not discounted how this may impact their work ethic compared to previous generations. The technological background that Gen Z will bring to the workforce is irreplaceable. This same background, however, also makes it so the generation understands the lack of communication many of their peers have developed due to the reliance of smartphones. Gen Z is aware of the risks that come with their different type of upbringing, but they believe that the ideas they will bring will counteract the negativities of the technological age. Gen Z is a new workforce that knows how they differ from those that came before them and is not afraid to recognize their weaknesses.

"The job search will be competitive."
"Technology opens doors."

We also wanted to know how members of Gen Z thought their job search would differ from previous generations. We asked them to tell us how they believe they will enter into the job market, and the responses represented the usual fears of anyone about to join the workforce.

The upcoming generation believes that they will struggle to find a dream job that fits their high level of education. They are greatly thankful for the opportunities they have been afforded when it comes to higher education, but they have started to realize that this may start to become a deficit in their lives due to the raised expectations by employers. There is more access to a vast network of potential employers due to technology, which can help the job search but hurt when recruiting top talent. It makes these "dream jobs" more difficult to obtain because they are no longer competing only with those in their immediate area or using real-life connections instead of services like LinkedIn.

Gen Z is also aware that their work environment will be much higher paced than those that came before them. There will be more technology involved and the entire culture will have to focus around this new world, rather than the one that their grandparents and parents grew up in. The fast-paced work environment is now one that Gen Z is not used to, however they will find themselves frustrated in many instances. The ability to have anything at any time thanks to Amazon, instant transfer, and other technological advances that represent the era can eventually lead to speed bumps in the work environment. Gen Z realizes that they are in this position, so the fast-paced work environment will be an adaptation needed to keep up with the changing world, but one that they will have to recognize in a cautious manner.

"Do It Myself"

While many organizations have learned how to create a culture in which Millennials can thrive, what Gen Z needs and wants can be quite different. There is a common theme of a "do it myself" attitude that arises in Gen Z in the workplace. Gen Z is looking for stability within the company in order to advance with given opportunities, whereas Millennials primarily crave safety, belonging, and working on what matters.

Jenkins (n.d.) notes:

> Seventy-five percent of Generation Z would be interested in a situation in which they could have multiple roles within one place of employment. Growing up in fast times and coming of age in an on-demand culture, Millennials have little patience for stagnation, especially when it comes to their careers. Generation Z won't want to miss out on any valuable experience and will want to flex their on-demand learning muscle by trying out various roles or projects (marketing, accounting, human resources, etc.) inside of the organization.
> 71% of Gen Z said they believe the phrase, "If you want it done right, then do it yourself." When given the option to arrange a group of desks, Millennials would opt for a collaborative arrangement and assemble the desks into a circle. Generation Z will be more competitive with their colleagues and will

harness a do-it-yourself mentality at work. In fact, 69 percent of Generation Z would rather have their own workspace than share it with someone else.

It is understood and quite apparent that Millennials don't necessarily want to work just for a paycheck, they want a purpose. They aspire to pursue their own development by receiving guidance from coaches, not a boss. Millennials are not interested in annual reviews, they want an ongoing conversation, not focusing on their weaknesses, but instead developing their strengths. They develop a collaborative mentality where everyone pitches in to work together.

Gen Z, on the other hand, establishes that money and job security are their top motivators in the workforce. Gen Z has a reputation and common theme of being impatient and often experiencing "Fear of Missing Out" (FOMO), so to help Gen Z's performance throughout the company, instant feedback is key. Their objective is to make a difference, but in reality, surviving and thriving is at the top of their priority list. Unlike Millennials, Gen Z prefers to be mentored rather than coached or bossed around in an environment in which they can advance quickly. They want to create a relationship with their leader in which there is honesty and transparency. Post-Millennials are notoriously known for being competitive. 72% of Gen Z said they are competitive with doing the same job and want to start their own business (Patel, 2017). In many case studies, it is shown that Gen Z wants to be assessed and judged based on their own merits and showcase their own individual talents.

Statistics and case studies suggest that the environment that Gen Z desires in a workplace is far different from that of Millennials. 69% of Gen Z would rather have their own space than share it with others in the workplace, and 71% say they live by the phrase, "if you want it done right, then do it yourself." Although Gen Z prefers the independent lifestyle in the workplace, 74% say they prefer to communicate face to face with colleagues, since they prefer a more personal approach. It is quite possible that Gen Z could constitute the ideal generation to strike the appropriate balance between online and offline workplace communications.

Gen Z (61%) has stronger desire for managers to listen to their ideas and value their opinions over Millennials (56%), and Millennials (58%) have a stronger desire for managers to allow them to work independently than Gen Z (46%) (Millennial Branding, 2014).

A 2016 Survey conducted by Lincoln Financial group tells us that Gen Z are far more optimistic than Millennials. In the workforce, Millennials tend to be more tolerant than Gen Z, since they have already encountered many more situations in life in which things could have the potential to go wrong. For Gen Z, on the other hand, it's all about getting the job done. It seems that good pay, positivity, and room to advance and grow are common themes as to what GeZ expects out of working in the workplace.

In Figure 1 below, it is clearly shown that the three desired job perks are pay (33.3%), benefits (11.9%), and environment (9.5%).

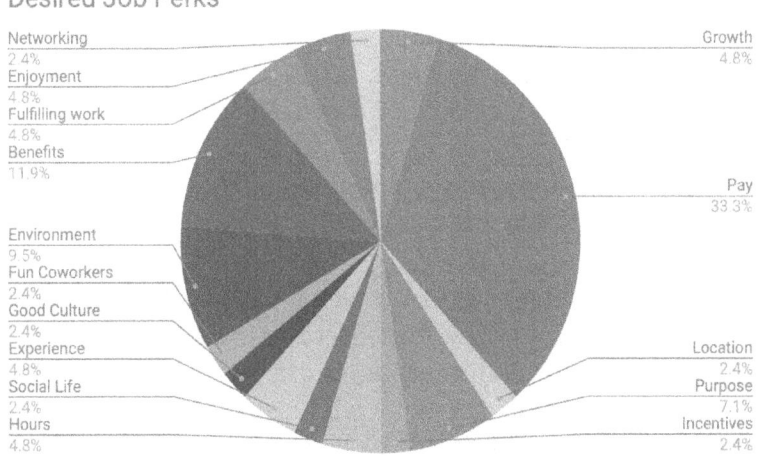

Desired Job Perks

Networking 2.4%
Enjoyment 4.8%
Fulfilling work 4.8%
Benefits 11.9%
Environment 9.5%
Fun Coworkers 2.4%
Good Culture 2.4%
Experience 4.8%
Social Life 2.4%
Hours 4.8%
Growth 4.8%
Pay 33.3%
Location 2.4%
Purpose 7.1%
Incentives 2.4%

Figure 1

In reference to the "do it myself" attitude, it is shown in Figure 2 below that 81.8% of the sample size prefers this attitude in the workforce.

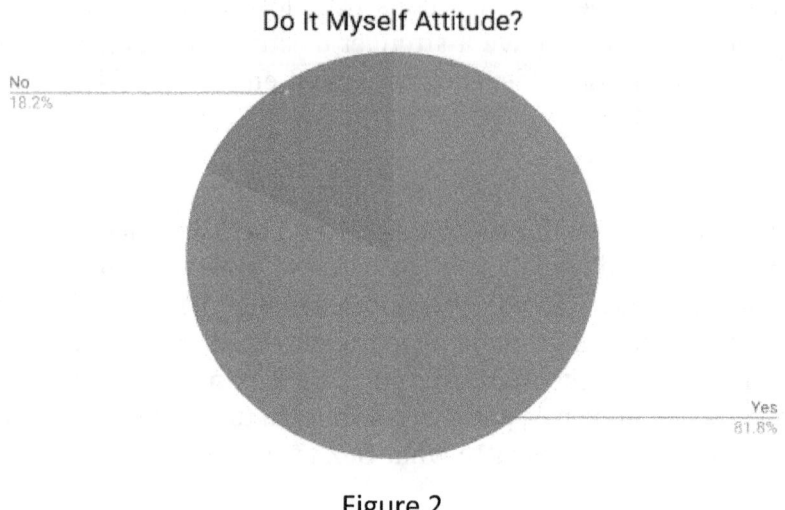

Do It Myself Attitude?

No
18.2%

Yes
81.8%

Figure 2

"Indifferent, Threatened, Good for Them"

Culturally, Gen Zers are ideal leaders in many ways, with the first being that they are connected. It is hard for someone who is a part of Gen Z to remember a time where they couldn't type a question into Google and find hundreds (if not thousands) of answers in less than a second. Technology also makes it easy for Gen Zers to voice their opinions to a large group of people and have potential to influence a lot of people.

Asked how they'd feel to have a Gen Z peer as their superior, a 20-year-old Gen Z student from Stevens Institute of Technology said, "I wouldn't really care as long as they earned it," which reflects more towards someone who respects their leader and can work for them peacefully.

Another Gen Z student, from Auburn University, answered the same question with, "That's ok because someone will always be better than you."

This type of answer can show someone who respects their leader but also someone who may not be as hard of a worker with that kind of attitude. Luckily for the workforce, however, most respondents to this question said they were fine with having a Gen Z leader and were supportive of the idea.

Out of all of our respondents, only 33% were a definite yes on being willing to relocate for a job. The other respondents were either a hard no or a maybe depending on their benefits, such as pay and which location. This could show more of a stubborn side of Gen Z, unwilling to go out of their comfort zone for a job opportunity, but it could also be a sign of a Gen Z's confidence in knowing they won't need to relocate for that job because they can get one where they are. On the contrast, those who are willing to relocate for work could just be willing to seize the opportunity to try something new.

"It depends on the job," said a 21-year-old student from Towson University.

This attitude could represent someone who can easily adapt to change and is willing to try something new. This could, in the long term, translate into someone who would one day be an effective leader. A combination of a Gen Z who is open to change such as a relocation but also confident in themselves could potentially combine into a very successful leader later in their work career.

Gen Z is going to be unique addition to the workforce, bringing new perspectives in the technological realm as well as different forms of collaboration. Their certainty in what they want and how they want it will lead to new retention and incentives at companies. The generation is ready to take on the working world and they know what they have to offer.

Millennials	Generation Z
Don't just work for a paycheck, they want a purpose.	Money and job security are their top motivators. They want to make a difference but surviving and thriving are more important.
They aren't pursuing job satisfaction, they are pursuing their own development.	They want to accumulate rewarding experiences. Gen Z tend towards being impatient and often experience FOMO (Fear Of Missing Out), so instant feedback and satisfaction are key.
They don't want bosses, they want coaches.	They want to be mentored in an environment where they can advance quickly. They want to look their leader in the eye and experience honesty and transparency.
They don't want annual reviews, they want ongoing conversations.	They don't want an annual work assessment, they want to be mentored and given feedback on an ongoing frequent (daily) basis.
They don't want to fix their weaknesses, they want to develop their strengths.	They were raised during the Great Recession and believe that there are winners and losers--and more people fall into the losing category. They want to have the tools to win, either through developing weaknesses or strengths.
They have a collaborative mentality where everyone pitches in and works together.	They are competitive. 72% of Gen Z said they are competitive with doing the same job. They are independent and want to be judged on their own merits and showcase their individual talents.
It's not just their job, it's their life.	Salary and benefits and how they can advance are pivotal. They are a DIY generation and they feel that other generations have overcomplicated the workplace.

Find more company culture resources at www.SmartTribesInstitute.com/FreeTools 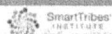 SmartTribes INSTITUTE

https://www.forbes.com/sites/christinecomaford/2017/04/22/what-generation-z-wants-from-the-workplace-are-you-ready/#5f52012553ef

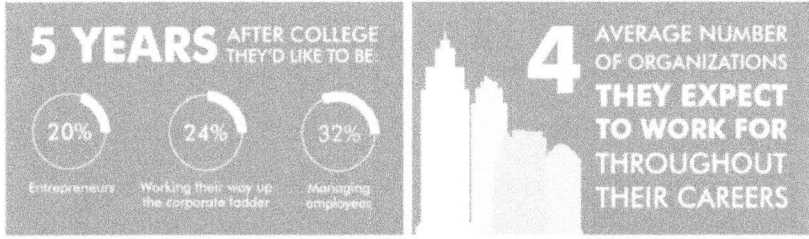

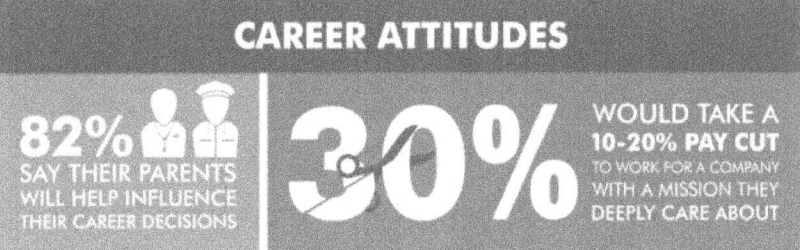

http://images.humanresourcesonline.net.s3.amazonaws.com/wp-content/uploads/2015/08/Robert-Half-Gen-Z-1-700x423.jpg

CHAPTER REFERENCES

Colletta, J. (2018). What Gen Z Wants from Work. Rertrieved May 2, 2019 from: http://hrexecutive.com/what-gen-z-wants-from-work/

Deloitte (2017). Generation Z will be Welcomed. Retrieved May 1, 2019 from: https://www2.deloitte.com/global/en/pages/about-deloitte/articles/millenni-al-survey-generation-z-welcomed.html

Jenkins, R. (n.d.)
Generation Z Versus Millennials: The 8 Differences You Need to Know. Retrieved May 2, 2019 from: https://www.inc.com/ryan-jenkins/genera-tion-z-vs-millennials-the-8-differences-you-.html

Millennial Branding (2014). Gen Y and Gen Z Global Workplace Expectations Study. Retrieved May 5, 2019 from http://millennialbranding.com/tag/gen-z/

Patel, D. (2017). 8 Ways Generation Z will Differe from Millenials in the Work-place. Retrieved May 2, 2019 from: https://www.forbes.com/sites/deeppa-tel/2017/09/21/8-ways-generation-z-will-differ-from-millennials-in-the-work-place/#6c5d45a376e5

Roujol, O. (2017). How Gen Z is Changing the World. Retrieved May 3, 2019 from: https://medium.com/@Odile_Roujol/how-Gen Z-is-changing-the-world-32ddo2bc23of

Scott, J. (2018). What Gen Z Wants from Work is Different than you might Thin. Retrieved May 2, 2019 from: https://www.tlnt.com/what-gen-z-wants-from-work-is-different-than-you-might-think/

GEN Z AUTHORS

BRIANNE SALERA
Brianne is currently a junior at Stevens Institute of Technology majoring in Finance with a minor in Quantitative Finance. Brianne is part of Generation Z and proud to be able to provide input on what the workplace looks like through the eyes of Gen Z.

SABRINA MOTIWALA
Sabrina is currently a junior at Stevens Institute of Technology majoring in Business and Technology with two concentrations in Finance and Information Systems. Sabrina is part of the 81.8% sample size in the "do it myself" attitude in the workforce.

JING WANG
Jing is currently a sophomore at Stevens Institute of Technology majoring in Business and Technology with concentrations in Computer Science and Information Systems. Jing is ready to embrace the new cultural changes and advancements as a member of Generation Z.

MOLLY DIGREGORY
Molly is currently a sophomore at Stevens Institute of Technology majoring in Business and Technology with a concentration in International Business. Molly believes that Gen Z is going to bring a completely new perspective to the workforce.

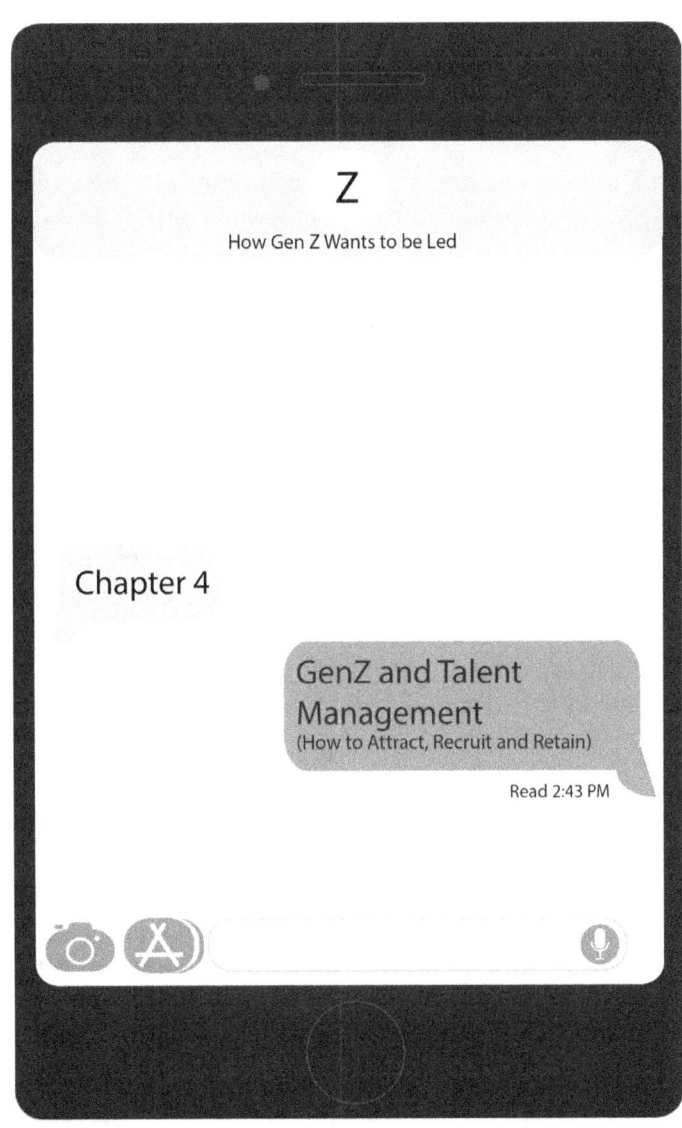

Z

How Gen Z Wants to be Led

Chapter 4

GenZ and Talent Management
(How to Attract, Recruit and Retain)

Read 2:43 PM

Good pay and positive corporate cultures are most likely to
attract both Millennials and Gen Z, but the keys to keeping
them happy are diversity, inclusion and flexibility.
(Friedman, 2018)

As Gen Z employees become more prominent in the workforce,
leadership perspectives within companies will have to evolve.
Gen Z is not only changing leadership perspectives within companies, but changing the methods of how a company attracts,
recruits and retains these Gen Z employees. This is extremely
important for businesses to understand if they want to attract
and retain top talent.

TALENT MANAGEMENT

Besides just having the proper skills to do a job, a company
wants their employees to fit in with the established organizational culture and reflect coporate values in the work that
they do. Just as companies look for a good fit within their firm,
employees do the same—especially Gen Z. Employees in this
generation are looking for a company that they can not only fit
in with culturally, but one that welcomes collaboration and allows for an entrepreneurial atmosphere. For a company looking
to not only attract, but retain Gen Z employees, it is essential
to get rid of antiquated technology and offer opportunities for
growth. These are just some of the ways Gen Z is changing the
expectations of companies, but before an organization focuses
on retaining Gen Z employees, we should first look at how to
recruit employees using the talent management process.

All things related to attracting and recruiting employees starts
with talent management. The human resources department
within an organization implements the daily activities of the
talent management process, which should ideally reflect the
entire company. The first process of the talent management
team is to clearly understand the company's goals and objec-

tives. The talent management team also has to plan the workforce. This means understanding what skills are essential to hire and what abilities can be trained. Both steps relate to each other, because to know what qualifications an employee needs, the talent management team has to understand the overall goals and objectives for the company.

Next, the company has to source and attract the talent. Sourcing talent means finding and networking with potential candidates for the job, such as using online job boards (Van Vulpen, 2018). Organizations have to ask why a skilled worker would want to work for them. When there are current employees that have been with the company for many years, it shows potential employees that there is a reason to be working for the company and opportunities for growth in their career. Gen Z wants to see that people have stayed with the company long-term and that its current employees are examples of that.

From talking with Gen Z employees who have recently been job searching, it is clear that they are concentrated on mentorship and growth opportunities within their companies. As one 22-year-old Gen Zer put it, "When I look at a place that I'd like to work, the first thing I look at is how long the average person is staying there. I want to work somewhere where there is room for growth, and not somewhere where people are leaving after a year because the only way they can advance is by leaving the company."

The learning and development stage of the talent management process provides this for employees. Although this step involves training new employees for their jobs to generate productive work, it also requires companies to build their employees' skills for the future. Skills development is essential to Gen Z employees as it trains them for their evolving job requirements and ultimately allows them to perform better and more efficiently. A company should put emphasis on this stage, it is extremely important to the Gen Z employees which can later help with retention (Van Vulpen, 2018).

Once the employees are hired and trained for their roles, a company's next step should be focusing on retaining them. If there is constant turnover within a company, it is challenging for daily business activities to be completed and there is a lack of consistency in the workplace (Van Vulpen, 2018). It makes it difficult for a company to focus on their bigger goals and the company vision when the company is concentrated on stopping a revolving door. This also wastes resources because a company is constantly using them for training new employees who only end up staying short-term. Long-term employees add great value to a company, not just through their work, but also through their attitude. Short-term employees can have a negative effect on office morale, making current employees question their job security.

Overall, employee retention promotes success for the company. With Gen Z employees, companies should focus on the benefits and growth they can provide. Gen Z employees are not as motivated by money as other generations, but are motivated by challenging work.

Performance management is the method through which a company ensures that employees are able to reach their work objectives and are executing their job responsibilities. Performance management is also a good tool to understand an employee's potential and see if an employee is able to handle greater responsibilities.

Promotion is the next step in the talent management process. Promotion within a company inspires employees and motivates them in their work. It also allows employees with their career development, which is an important job aspect for Gen Z. Another 22-year-old student noted, "By allowing opportunities for advancement within the company, it makes me feel like I'm working somewhere that values its people and works to keep them, and not like I need to be constantly thinking about my next career move and where I'm going to work next."

One of the main aspects Gen Z employees look for is professional development within a company, making the promotion stage a great way to retain employees. Most people do not want to work in the same exact job for long periods of time. This step works closely with career planning for employees that are performing well and handling their responsibilities. An organization should provide recognition and rewards to these employees which also motivate them to continue to stay and work for the company.

The final stage in the talent management process is succession planning. This step is about the talent management team deciding who will replace employees when they leave due to situations such as retirement or employees who have a higher position. It is essential for organizations to be ready and have in mind people candidates who can replace top management when the time comes. Being prepared for the replacement allows the business to continue at the same pace (Van Vulpen, 2018).

A great talent management process is able to attract the top talent to your company and retain these employees to develop their professional careers. The next generation of employees for all of these companies will be Gen Z. When searching for the next top talent of Gen Z employees, we have to first start with understanding how to attract them.

ATTRACTING GEN Z TO AN ORGANIZATION

Companies are starting to realize that Gen Z comprise a distinct breed of employees, different from any that came before them. Compared to Millennials, this demographic has unique values, priorities, and work outlooks. Estimated to represent 75% of the workforce by 2030 (Fatemi, 2018), Gen Z undoubtedly is the future of the American economy. The big question that companies now have to ask themselves is, "How can we effective ly attract this new generation of modern-minded and unique workers?"

Perhaps more than any generation that preceded it, Gen Z cares about the society and our planet.
"It's about more than the money for us...we're here to make real change," says Alvin Varghese, a marketing student at Temple University.

Members of Gen Z want to make their mark, in part, by making our society better than past generations have managed to do. According to a 2017 survey by Cone Communications, 94% of Gen Z believes companies ought to address social and environmental issues, as compared to 87% of Millennials and 86% of the general population. In fact, according to a 2015 report from Robert Half Inc., 30% of Gen Z are willing to take a 10-20% pay cut if it means they are able to work towards a mission they care about (Fatemi, 2018).

In order to attract this new influx of workers, companies are going to need to make strides in their corporate social responsibility (CSR). Companies that place an emphasis on CSR will naturally attract Gen Z workers who want to make a difference, rather than just make a living. Numerous companies have already realized this potential competitive advantage and have doubled down on their CSR programs. IBM, Google, Johnson & Johnson, and Netflix are just some of the big corporations that have placed emphasis on CSR. Google allows its workers to devote up to 20 hours of work time to volunteer efforts each year and awards $50 grants to nonprofit organizations for every five hours that a Googler spends volunteering.

Gen Z grew up during the technological age. They were tethered to tech gadgets and have experienced the social media boom. They've spent more time glued to their screens and less time outdoors, socializing and developing a social support system, than their Millennial predecessors. Although more research needs to be carried out on the subject, initial studies point to the conclusion that Gen Z is more likely to experience depression and other mental health disorders compared to previous generations. For this reason, Gen Z will be partial to employers that offer strong mental support services to their employees. "Companies that have mental health initiatives definitely have an advantage. I personally would feel more comfortable working for a company that offers services because that tells me that they view me as a human being, and not just an employee," said Heather, a computer science student at Drexel University.

According to research by Lovell Corporation (2017), while Millennials are more likely to prioritize employability supports such as education, training, career support, etc., Gen Z is more likely to gravitate towards mental health support as a top priority. Companies with well-organized mental health support systems, such as company-sponsored yoga classes or access to personal counseling sessions, will be more successful in this area than companies who don't. Many larger companies have found a solution in offering or incentivizing subscriptions to online therapy apps. These apps are a great step in the right direction and appeal to the tech-savvy Gen Z demographic.

Another important difference between Gen Z and employees of previous generations is their inclination toward engaging in entrepreneurial pursuits. Research suggests that, as a whole, Gen Z is much more creative and entrepreneurial-minded than past generations (McDowell, 2018). Gen Z has realized the thrill of exploring new and unfamiliar areas, and of acquiring skills that will equip them to pursue their specific passions. In addition, they have grown up surrounded by entrepreneurial inspirations like Steve Jobs, Mark Zuckerberg, or Jeff Bezos, who reached worldwide stardom and are conceptualized by the media as celebrities.

"We've grown up in an era where successful entrepreneurs are glorified, as they should be," said Parsh Jain, a quantitative finance major at Stevens Institute of Technology. "It's the ulti-mate dream...it represents everything that Gen Z strives for in terms of creative pursuits."

If organizations hope to be competitive in terms of attracting Gen Z talent, they must create environments that make possible the channeling of the entrepreneurial spirit within the confines of an organization. This is not a simple task by any means. A recent study found that while 75% of large companies consider themselves to be entrepreneurial, 75% of entrepreneurs leave employers because they don't feel they have the opportunity to be entrepreneurial. Unless policies and practices change, this trend is destined to get much worse with the rise of Gen Z in the workplace.

Some companies, including 3M and Dreamworks, have suc-cessfully implemented entrepreneurship into the workplace. Both of these companies permit employees to set aside a fixed percentage of on-the-job time to pursue ideas and endeavors that are unrelated to their primary jobs. Even smaller-scale ini-tiatives, such as company-wide "Hackathons" that encourage entrepreneurial spirit can move waters and attract Gen Z. The valuable members of Gen Z are growing up by the day. They are no longer children and will dominate the workforce in the very near future. At the end of the day, companies have to be pre-pared to do what it takes to attract this demographic as soon as possible. The "first movers" will gain a competitive advantage and enjoy success.

RECRUITING GEN Z TO AN ORGANIZATION

In order to recruit Gen Z, companies need to deliver an excep-tional candidate experience. Gen Z is much less likely than old-er generations to do business with a company where they have had a poor experience as a job applicant. Companies must iden-tify any potential problems, even things like non-mobile-friend-ly career pages and slow communications and work toward creating an effortless, timely, and relevant candidate experience. A new generation requires updated recruiting tactics, which is why companies should utilize innovative technologies.

One such example is Pymetrics, which uses neuroscience games and bias-free artificial intelligence to predictively match people with jobs where they'll perform at the highest levels. Google Hire is another recruiting app that helps distribute job listings, identify candidates, build relationships, and manage the interview process. Mya and Wade & Wendy are a few services that offer chatbots that automate the process from resume to interview. Innovative recruiting tools such as these can give companies a competitive advantage when recruiting Gen Z.

Lastly, companies should be actively managing their employer brand on sites like Glassdoor.com. A whopping 70% percent of candidates look to company reviews before they make career decisions and 69% are likely to apply to a job if the employer actively manages its employer brand. Employers can manage their brand by responding to reviews, updating their profile, and sharing updates on the work environment. With over 10 million of the 32 million monthly users on Glassdoor being Millennials and Gen Z, it's a must that companies leverage the service. One company that has bought into the managing its brand is SAP, who has a dedicated employee, whose full-time job is to monitor Glassdoor, where they look at reviews, respond to reviews, and act on trends and/or feedback.

RETAINING GEN Z TO AN ORGANIZATION

Three main elements that Gen Z employees look at when deciding whether to stay with a company are benefits, work structure, and after-work social gatherings. According to Friedman (2018), 43% of Millennials plan to quit their current job within two years. Only 28% plan to stay in their current role for more than five years. The survey is based on the views of 10,455 Millennials and 1,844 members of Gen Z, questioned across

36 countries. Because of this, each employer has to provide a good reason for people to stay. Without a meticulous plan that makes Gen Z employees excited to work for the company, turnover rates can skyrocket.

The most notable benefits that Gen Z employees look for are training opportunities, insurance, paid leave, vacation days, food, laundry, and after-work social gatherings. Many companies such as Google, Facebook, and Apple have been implementing a lot of these benefits into their structures.

Gen Zers want to have everything taken care of, so that they do not have to worry about it during work.

Gen Z Student, Age 18 - Stevens Institute of Technology

Another factor upon which Gen Z employees agree unanimously is work structure. Sitting at a cubicle all day is not going to fly anymore. Having an open floor plan is now the rule, not the exception. In addition to having an open floor plan to encourage open collaboration, it is expected for there to be different training opportunities, face-to-face interactions, rotational work groups, and mentorship.

"Gen Z staff want to make sure that they are welcome at work and that they have some sort of identity at work."

Gen Z, Age 20

This is only achieved when they have a chance to prove themselves to their boss and there is no office politics at play. If the latter is the case, people will not want to be genuine for fear of being ostracized by their peers.

Gen Z also wants to have the opportunity to participate in social gatherings after work. Having the chance to talk and interact with associates makes people loosen up and gives them the option of converse about other aspects of their life like hobbies, vacation ideas, and stories.

Gen Z Student, Age 19 - Stevens Institute of Technology

People want to bring their most genuine selves forward, and social gatherings at restaurants and bars afford employees the chance to do that. Although typically not mandated by the company and often more informal and group-specific, it is a start.

As Gen Z's expectations are changing, companies are changing with them, from leadership to talent management teams. Companies have been evolving their methods of attracting, recruiting and retaining Gen Z employees. When searching for jobs, Gen Z is more focused on high-tech companies with an entrepreneurial atmosphere. Gen Z also looks for companies with a great work structure and benefits.

CAPTURING SOME KEY STATISTICS TO CONSIDER IN TRYING ATTRACT, RECRUIT AND RETAIN GEN ZERS:

- 34% are most motivated by opportunities for advancement, followed by more money (27%) and meaningful work (23%).

- 41% want to work at midsize organizations as the ideal work environment, followed by large organizations (38%). [Robert Half]

- 28% said balancing work and personal obligations was the top future career concern, followed by making enough money (26%) and finding a stable job (23%). [Robert Half]

- 60% want to have an impact on the world with their jobs (compared to 39% of Millennials). [Intern Sushi / CAA]

- 41% of Gen Z say corporate offices are their workplace preference [Future Workplace / Randstad]

- Technologies that Gen Z want their employers to incorporate into the workplace include: social media (41%), wearables (27%) and virtual reality (26%). [Future Workplace / Randstad]

- The top employee benefits Gen Z desires include work flexibility (19%), healthcare coverage (15%) and training (14%). [Future Workplace / Randstad]

- 34% are most concerned about boosting their people management skills. [Vision Critical]

- 93% say that a company's impact on society affects their decision to work there. [i4cp]

https://danschawbel.com/blog/39-of-the-most-interesting-facts-about-generation-z/

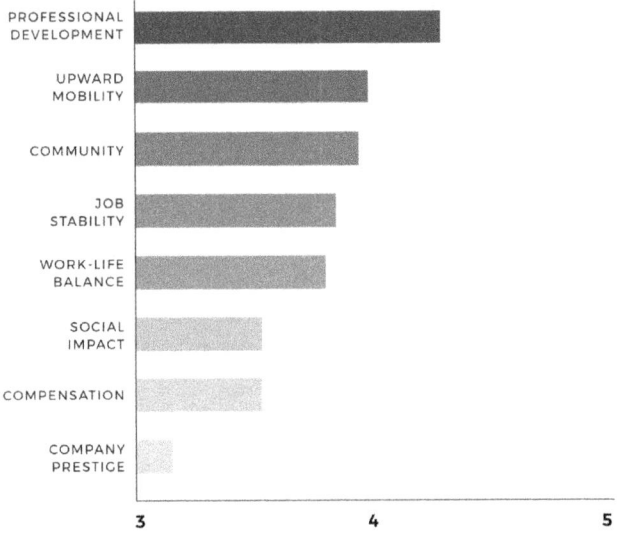

WHAT GEN Z WANTS
OVERALL

RIPPLEMATCH

https://ripplematch.com/journal/article/a-comprehensive-look-at-what-generation-z-wants-in-the-workplace-fa8o8aco/

https://advisory.kpmg.us/content/dam/advisory/en/pdfs/generation-z-talent.pdf

Based on the current understanding of Generation Z's characteristics, organizations should consider implementing or revamping the following talent management programs:

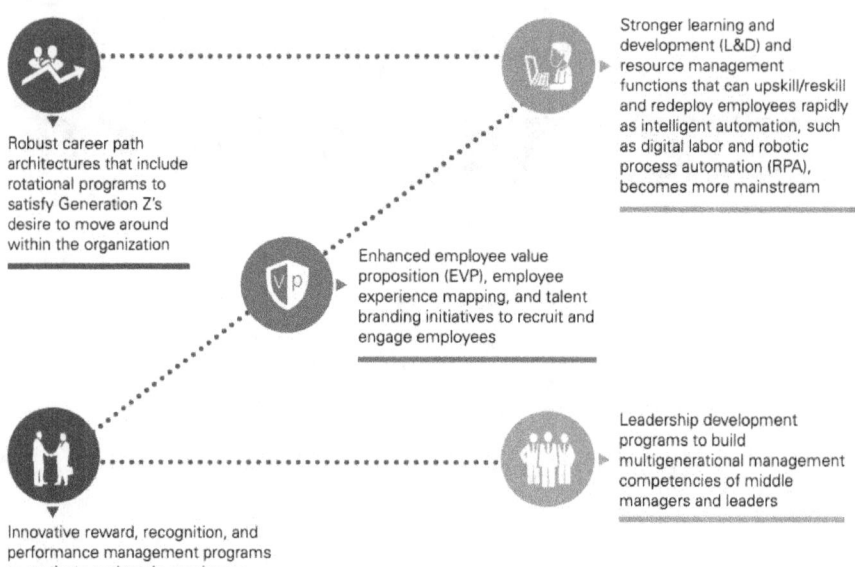

Robust career path architectures that include rotational programs to satisfy Generation Z's desire to move around within the organization

Stronger learning and development (L&D) and resource management functions that can upskill/reskill and redeploy employees rapidly as intelligent automation, such as digital labor and robotic process automation (RPA), becomes more mainstream

Enhanced employee value proposition (EVP), employee experience mapping, and talent branding initiatives to recruit and engage employees

Innovative reward, recognition, and performance management programs to motivate and retain employees

Leadership development programs to build multigenerational management competencies of middle managers and leaders

https://advisory.kpmg.us/content/dam/advisory/en/pdfs/generation-z-talent.pdf

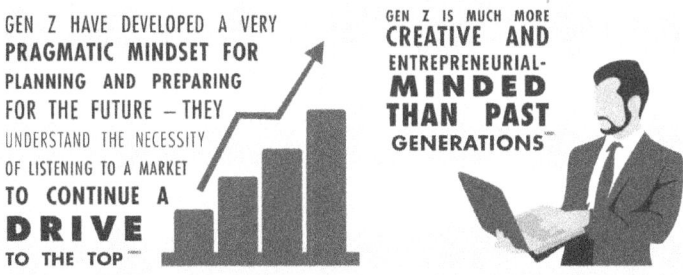

https://www.silverswanrecruitment.com/recruiting-and-retaining-gen-z-workers-in-2019/

CHAPTER REFERENCES

Cone Communications (2017). 2017 Cone Communication CSR Study. Retrieved May 3, 2019 from http://www.conecomm.com/research-blog/2017-csr-study

Fatemi, F. (2108). What's Your Strategy for Attracting Generation Z? Retrieved May 1, 2019 from: https://www.forbes.com/sites/falonfatemi/2018/03/31/whats-your-strategy-for-attracting-generation-z/#19afd3166cad

Friedman, Z. (2018). 43% Of Millennials Plan to Quit Their Job Within 2 Years. Retrieved May 6, 2019 from: https://www.forbes.com/sites/zackfriedman/2018/05/22/millennials-quit-job/#988f49257f14

Lovell Corporation (2017). The Change Generation Report. Retrieved May 3, 2019 from https://www.lovellcorporation.com/the-change-generation-report/

McDowell, J. (2018) The World of Gen Z. Retrieved May 1, 2019 from: https://issuu.com/joshmcdowellministry/docs/the_world_of_gen_z_portfolio_final_

Van Vulpen, E. "A Comprehensive Guide to Building a Talent Management Process." Digital HR Tech Blog, 19 Dec. 2018, www.digitalhrtech.com/talent-management-process/.

GEN Z AUTHORS

OLIVIA RYKER
Olivia is currently a junior at Stevens Institute of Technology and is studying marketing. As a member of Generation Z, Olivia is looking forward to building the future of marketing. She is excited about being able to make a difference in the workplace and redefining what it means to be in marketing.

DAVID SMOLYAK
David is currently a sophomore at Stevens Institute of Technology majoring in Finance with a minor in Quantitative Finance. As a part of Generation Z, David is hoping to grow in the field of finance. He is thrilled to change some of the stereotypes that are prevalent in the financial services workplace and provide others with a more dynamic work experience based on his findings.

SASHANK SINDHIA
Sashank is currently a Freshman at Stevens Institute of Technology majoring in Business & Technology. Sashank is excited about entering the workforce in a few years and establishing his career. As a member of Gen Z, he understands that he has a skillset different than generations that preceded him, and he is ready to use his talents to create a difference.

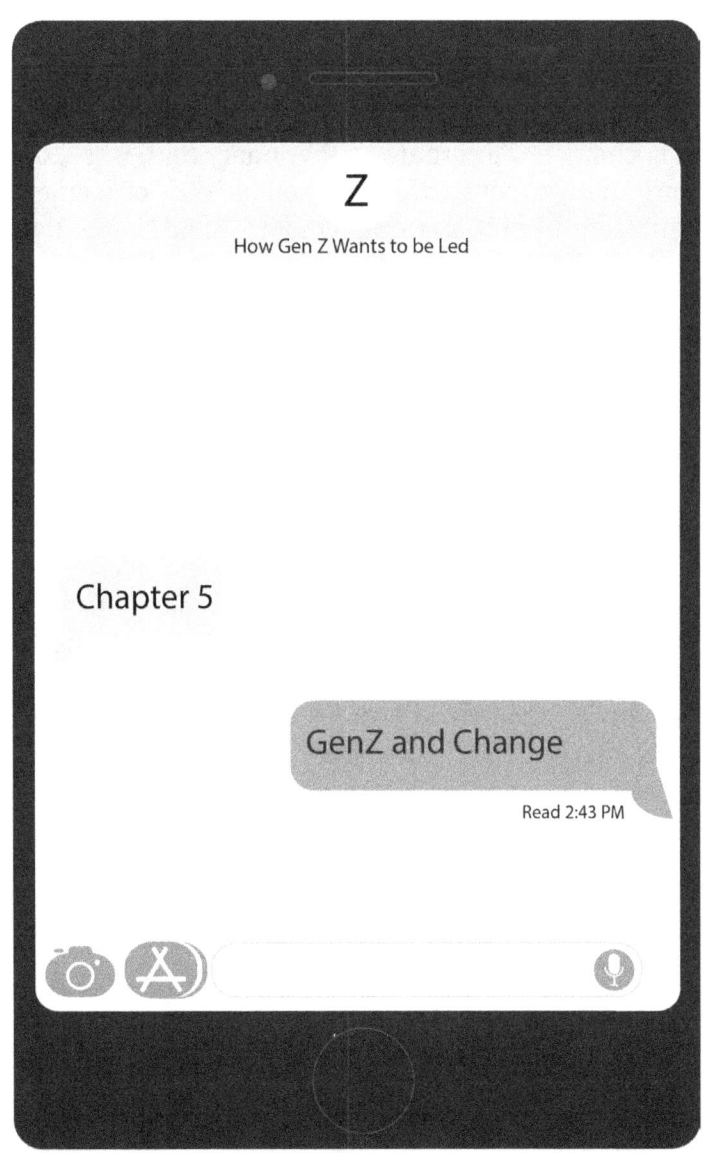

Z

How Gen Z Wants to be Led

Chapter 5

GenZ and Change

Read 2:43 PM

"Some of the biggest changes Generation Z faces today would be technological and cultural."

Gen Z, Age 21

What is change? According to Dictionary.com, it is "to make the form, nature, content, future course, etc., of [something] different from what it is or from what it would be if left alone." This definition is a very broad one; essentially change means to alter something. Something—or *someone,* we should add—was once in one state, and now is in a completely different one. But what does change mean for Gen Z?

" I remember watching a trailer recently for a movie, where the trailer showed a Blockbuster Video in it, and the producers came at it from a sort of nostalgic angle like 'hey, remember this gem?' But it was very powerful for me because I did say to myself, 'That's right! Blockbuster used to be a thing! I've been to one before!' Of course, they are all gone now for the most part, but those younger than me will not know what a Blockbuster was. Just like how I didn't know what a Rolodex was or what life was like before you could press control-F on textbooks to find what you were looking for. It made me feel old."

Gen Z, Age 21

This is a great example of technological change, because it was not that long ago that something like Blockbuster was a seemingly booming business, but because of the rise of new technology and advancements into the online streaming space, Blockbuster quickly became a thing of the past. Things like this can happen in the workforce, with things such as computers, machinery, and even people.

*"In the finance industry, a lot of companies seem to be hiring
people with technical and STEM backgrounds. People like
engineers, computer scientists, and mathematicians are all being
looked at because of the advancements in technology. Business
is done in different ways than it used to be and the industry is
calling for this type of analytical person."*

Gen Z, Age 21

Once a member of Gen Z enters into the workforce, they have
to be prepared for changes. For example, in approximately 1.5
years, technology will be affected and/or changed, every 3
years there will be some substantial organizational changes,
and within 8 years there are major workforce turnovers (Dool,
2019).

Other than technological and organizational changes, Gen Z
faces cultural changes throughout the workplace as well. First
off, Gen Zers will be very mobile in the workplace. This means
that Gen Z will not be confined to an office space, and that they
will be on the move, overseas, and at home, all while working.
Three-in-five employees currently state they do not need to be
physically present at the office to be productive. (Dool, 2019). Is
this a good thing though?

*"Sure, of course it is a positive to be mobile and productive. It
also makes me happier being able to work in settings I may feel
more comfortable and productive in other than a cubicle. On
the flip side though, being out on the road and traveling a lot for
work, or even working from places that are supposed to be seen
as a 'no work zone,' such as your own home or something, could
be a negative. Some people may want to leave their work at the
office, and completely forget about it when they walk through
their front door. In terms of travelling, it may be hard for Gen Z*

to date or even start families if they are away from home for long intervals."

Gen Z, Age 21

Another cultural change facing Gen Z is the rise in diversity amongst firms. One individual states,

"Diversity is an important asset that firms can have, because it is valuable for a firm to have diversity of thought. People coming from different backgrounds can add new perspectives and can lead to new solutions for problems that organizations face. Sometimes this could be a daunting culture shock for some people, but I think for the most part, our generation accepts diversity as the norm and the future. I think we see great value in diversity of thought and know how to use it to our advantages."

Gen Z, Age 21

The constant need to become accustomed to new technology is normalized in Gen Zers' lives due to the pace of technological advancement over the past twenty years. During the generation's lifetime, music has transitioned from physical CDs to streaming services, McDonald's went from people taking orders to screens taking them, and video gaming has gone from block figures to virtual reality. GenX sees such change as a part of life—something they don't question.

While older generations may have had trouble integrating technology into their work, usually due to lack of experience with it, most everyone in Gen Z has a smartphone and feels they need this technology to operate normally in their daily lives. This in turn makes them more adept at adapting to new technology in the workplace. Not only has this prepared them for technological change in the future, it also allowed many to connect and share information, removing a sense of mystery and awe about the world and what is defined as success.

This connected awareness among members of the generation is what spawned the current trend in office culture toward a focus on teamwork and less on hierarchy. This is the continuation of a trend that has effectively began in the 1960's, as more women and international employees joined the corporate ranks, and people began to wear more casual attire in the workplace. In reaction, management implemented the cubicle setup, which proved incredible unpopular as the years when on. In fact, a 1997 study asserted that 97% of people who worked in cubicles wanted to switch work places (Cain, 2018).

Now, by merging the ideas of a more inclusive and casual workplace and a universal disapproval of cubicles, the popular office trend right now is open office spaces, and team-oriented work. Another part of work culture for Gen Z is the propensity to keep moving jobs, something they do much more frequently than previous generations. However, this also comes from their nature of wanting more instant gratification than previous generations. The workplace is longer dominated by Baby Boomers, but shared between them and Generation X, Millennials, and the rising Gen Z.

"As Generation Z, we grew up in the post-9/11 world. We're accustomed to terrorism, economic turbulence, and a divided world. It's what makes us strong proponents of change."

Gen Z, Age 22

Consequently, offices are experiencing an increased proportion of older employees (Baby Boomers), who hold a significant percentage of managerial, executive and other senior-level positions. This generation is known for working long hours and has most likely been at their employer for most if not all of their working career and they may be less adaptive to ongoing workplace changes.

"During the past few decades, technology, cultural sensitivity and workplace environments have transformed the workplace into one that I barely recognize."

Baby Boomer, Age 61

In 1954, the typical American woman was a housewife (Gordon, 2004). That is certainly no longer the case, with more than 60 percent of American women now part of the workforce. Nearly all major corporations now have female executives, half of the Forbes 500 companies have female corporate officers, and eight have female CEOs. There is no question that these numbers will rise as more talented women reach their career peaks.

This shift toward inclusivity has not just been confined to women, either. Ever since the 1970s, minorities and handicapped individuals have increasingly formed a part of the corporate workforce. This reflects a reformed mindset geared towards human optimization, workplace flexibility and retention, and not to mention the boon to ingenuity and creativity (Dool, 2019). As the demographics have changed, so too have toxic elements of may have hindered this shift in the past. Some once-common workplace behaviors, such as smoking and drinking in the office, are now restricted or no longer tolerated.

"Everyone smoked at work, even doctors in their offices. My boss would not have lasted long either today, as he frequently drank scotch in his office "

Silent Generation, Age 77

This mentality of change has made the workplace a more comfortable environment in which to work. Sexual harassment training is almost universally mandatory, along with other forms of sensitivity training, to clamp done on inappropriate conduct. Cooperation is vital for any business to succeed, and that can not be done without some form of respect for one another.

In the past, businesses needed bosses—the leaders who determined everything regarding a company's direction: An organizational structure with a central command organization and a rigid top-to-bottom hierarchy.

"Orders were given and you worked independently. You'd really interact with someone only if more than one department was needed and you had question or concern."

Baby Boomer, Age 60

"I feel that Gen Z is in the best position for group work and collaboration. After all, we spent our entire school careers doing group projects and learning to play well with others."

Gen Z, Age 20

Group projects and the evolving nature of the manager create an environment in which Gen Z is well suited to flourish. "They crave conversation and dialogue and they want responsibility and will look to management for guidance" (Kelly, 2017).

Gen Z works well in small groups, with highly defined goals and leaders establishing a clear chain of command and communication that will help bring out the best. Gen Z expects good work to be rewarded, because of thei need for instant gratification. Pretty much every member of the generation grew up with the "participation trophy" mentality, and it's still in full bloom. While they don't expect to get something just for showing up as we enter the workplace, we nevertheless like to be recognized, even for small accomplishments.

"I love getting praise from my boss! It keeps me motivated."

Gen Z, Age 23

This also showcases another growing workplace trend mentioned earlier: bosses showing a greater interest in their employees' work and monitoring their progress. Organizations with viable rewards programs will meet expectations and encourage growth in performance. Companies should make sure to praise effort and reward actual results. Gen Z is expected to change their job several times within 10 years, because they thrive on opportunity. They experienced a childhood where our parents were exposed to layoffs and downsizing, so they subconsciously desire strong financial opportunities. It's natural for them to be self-sustaining and not have to rely on others to help them when living on their own. After all, they get a lot of ire from older generations for being coddled and relying on their parents for help, so they feel have something to prove.

Companies that want to retain Gen Z workers should be able to show them where, when, and how their dream position is attainable within the company. The old ways are no longer productive in a highly-connected, intensely-competitive business environment. Managers should lead from behind, and encourage their teams to innovate. Sure, technology increases productivity, but business success is built on the people who contribute their talents and knowledge to that success. Who better to yield and cultivate the new knowledge and technology than the freshest minds who are the most familiar with it? Businesses need to invest in the digital tools employees need, but also hire the best, too. People, not technology, build business success.

72% of current high school students want to start their own business someday. Already, 34% of U.S. workers are freelancers, and the gig economy shows signs of continued growth (Leading Tomorrow, 2018). Growing up in the age of the Internet, Gen Z has unprecedented access to information. Unlike any generation before them, they can engage the broader world at an early age. In addition to being tech-savvy, they possess a healthy sense of curiosity and have the tools to pursue their interests and find information quickly.

"When I don't know something, I Google it, and it's why people think I'm smart."

Gen Z, Age 19

Because of the vast technological tools available at their fingertips, Gen Z feels empowered to act independently. Gen Z is proving to be practical and self-focused in their views of the future. One benefit of this is that they see the need for long-term goals and are often willing to sacrifice in the moment for future security.

While Gen Z is set to inherit the world, older generations remain fearful of handing over the keys.

"In our generation, we valued relationships and did not grow up with technology running our lives."

Baby Boomer, Age 60

Baby Boomers grew up making phone calls and writing letters. This enabled them to develop and solidify strong interpersonal skills. They became fluent in technology and now use cell phones and tablets because they were fully grown and witnessed the first implementations. The difference is that they tended to use these technologies as productivity tools as opposed to connectivity tools, an idea that mainly came with Millennials.

"Machines are just tools to do our bidding. I remember when computers were the size of offices and were used for calculations, not emails."

Baby Boomer, Age 62

The older generations like to group Gen Z and Millennials together, which unfortunately associates both with negative stereotypes. The younger generations are seen as pushy, unyielding, and spoiled and the above mentioned qualities are glanced over; however, Gen Z are more concerned about being part of a bigger cause and a part of something that really matters. They are not afraid to work, and they don't see the need to distinguish between work and a personal life. When it comes to change, they expect it.

Generations at a Glance

	Baby Boomers 1946-1964	Gen Xers 1965-1977	Gen Yers 1978-1989	Gen Zers 1990-1999
Behavior	Challenge the rules	Change the rules	Create the rules	Customize the rules
Training	Preferred in moderation	Required to keep me	Continuous and expected	Ongoing and essential
Learning style	Facilitated	Independent	Collaborative and networked	Technology-based
Communication style	Guarded	Hub and spoke	Collaborative	Face-to-face
Problem-solving	Horizontal	Independent	Collaborative	Entrepreneurial
Decision-making	Team informed	Team included	Team decided	Team persuaded
Leadership style	Unilateral	Coach	Partner	Teaching
Feedback	Once per year, during the annual review	Weekly/daily	On demand	Consistent and frequent
Change management	Change = caution	Change = opportunity	Change = improvement	Change = expected

Sources: • The Changing Workforce: Urgent Challenges and Strategies, 2007, Joe Kraus, associate partner, Human Capital Management Practice, IBM. • Bruce Tulgan, Nichoel Rainmaker Thinking

https://recruitloop.com/blog/what-you-need-to-know-when-recruiting-generation-z/

CHAPTER REFERENCES

Cain, Á. (2018). The progression of office culture from the 50s to today. Retrieved May 1, 2019 from: https://www.businessinsider.com/office-culture-then-and-now-2018-5#saval-wrote-that-in-1997-steelcase-survey-found-93-of-participants-who-worked-in-cubicles-wanted-to-switch-workspaces-28

Dictionary.com (2019). Change. Retrieved May 3, 2019 from: https://www.dictionary.com/browse/change

Dool, R. (2019). The Functions of Management in the 21st Century. Principles of Management. Stevens Institute of Technology, Hoboken. Lecture.

Dool, R. (2019). What is 'Management. Principles of Management. Stevens Institute of Technology, Hoboken. Lecture.
Gordon, J. (2004). The 50 Biggest Changes In The Last 50 Years. Retrieved from https://www.americanheritage.com/50-biggest-changes-last-50-years

Kelly, M. (2017). When Generation Z Hits the Workplace. Retrieved May 3, 2019 from https://productiveleaders.com/when-generation-z-hits-the-workplace/

Leading Tomorrow (2018). 3 Strengths of Gen Z. Retrieved May 2, 2019 from https://www.leadingtomorrow.org/blog/3-strengths-of-gen-z

GEN Z AUTHORS

MARK TENBRINK

Mark is currently a senior at Stevens Institute of Technology where he is majoring in Quantitative Finance with a concentration in finance and economics. Mark is one of the last generations to be born in the 20th century where he has seen pivotal changes in consumer technology which affect his experiences in the modern workforce. He will be entering into the consulting world shortly after graduation and will put his knowledge to good use in an ever changing work environment.

MATTHEW GOETZ

Matthew is currently a junior at Stevens Institute of Technology and he is majoring in Business and Technology with concentrations in Finance and Information Systems with a minor in Economics. Matthew is a member of Generation Z and is enthusiastic about being a forerunner of documentation for his generation coming of age and entering the workplace. He believes this research and participation is vital in his pursuit of project management employment opportunities.

CHARLES LAPOLLA

Charles is currently a junior at Stevens Institute of Technology where he is majoring in Finance with a minor in Quantitative Finance. Growing up always on the cusp of new innovations, Charles is excited to go into the workforce and see how the finance landscape constantly adapts to new market behaviors impacted by the advancement of technology.

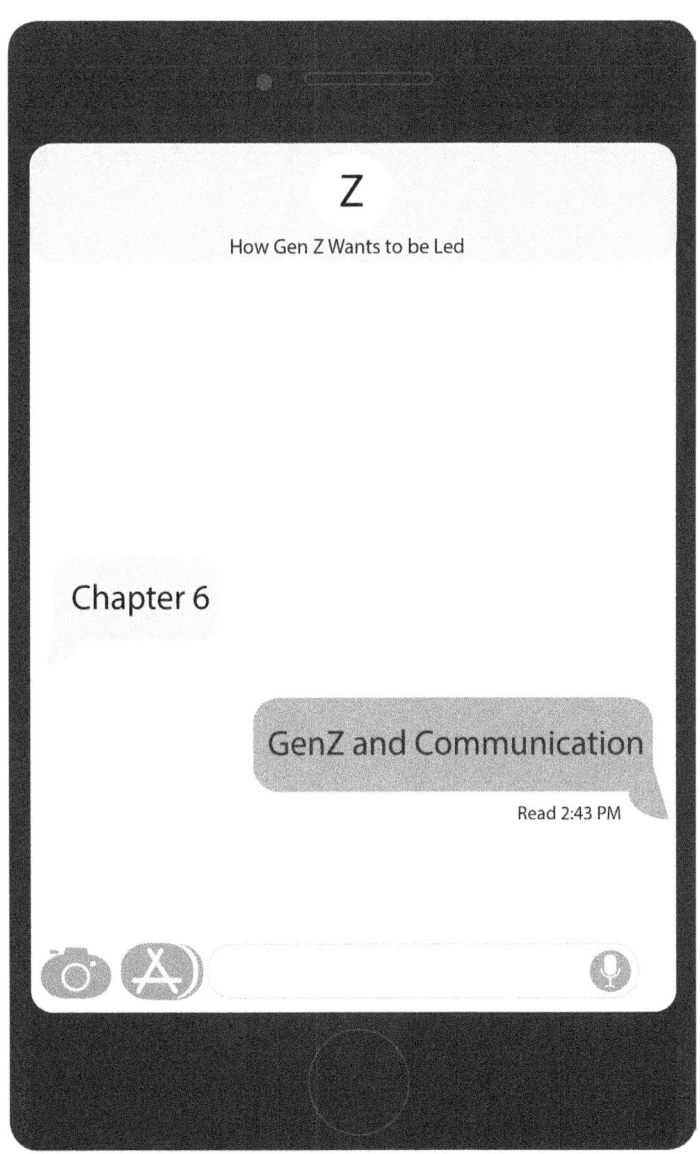

Z

How Gen Z Wants to be Led

Chapter 6

GenZ and Communication

Read 2:43 PM

*"I can simultaneously create a document, edit it, post a photo
on Instagram and talk on the phone, all from the user-friendly
interface of my iPhone. Generation Z takes in information
instantaneously, and loses interest just as fast."*
Gen Z, Age 18 (Hughes, 2018)

Communication is a vital aspect of leadership. While it
might seem like a very simple trait, many leaders today
lack good communication skills and their companies suffer as a result. In fact, businesses with as few as 100 employees spend, on average, 17 hours each week clarifying
previous communications, which translates to an annual
cost of at least $525,000 (Russo, n.d.). Therefore, it is im-
perative that Gen Z master effective communication in order to become great leaders. This chapter will explain the
certain aspects of communication required to achieve this
standard.

The main purpose of communication is to talk with other people about accomplishing tasks or to inform others
about details. Communication has many definitions but it
can be defined as the process of creating or sharing meaning in informal conversation, group interaction, or public
speaking. The *Random House Dictionary* defines communication as the interchange of thoughts, in which people
share opinions and various information. Being an effective communicator results in an ability to solve problems,
increase productivity, and decrease stress.

Relationships between workers and managers play a vital
role in effective communication. Studies show that close
relationships between managers and employers often result in better communication. A manager should be open
to discussion and listen to their employees' opinions on
how the company or firm can run more efficiently. Managers must be capable and must be relied on to lead a team
of workers to attain the company's goals. With this being said, it is the manager's responsibility to use effective

communication to establish unity and teamwork in completing projects. As Rollo May (n.d.), an American psychologist said, "Strong Communication leads to community, that is, to understanding, intimacy and mutual valuing."

When employers have strained relationships with a manager, it usually affects the company's production. According to a study, one of the most popular complaints about managers is that they talk too much when they are trying to get their point across. Another complaint that employees have is favoritism. Victor Lipman (2015) author of the book, "The Type B Manager," states, "Georgetown University's business school in 2011 surveyed senior executives at companies with over 1,000 employees, and found that 84% admitted favoritism "takes place at their own organizations."

Managers need to show equal treatment in regards to praising the efforts of employees. As a manager, making sure an employee is excited to get up and go to work is essential in ensuring a successful operation. Favoring one worker over another can create division in the workplace, so managers must ensure that each employee's hard work is not going unnoticed. This style of communication makes employees feel that their voice is being heard, that they are important, and that they have the support of their boss.

In today's generation, technology keeps emerging at an erratic rate. Different forms of technology have increased the many forms of communication that exist in the world today. The emergence of technologies and social media, the advancement of email servers, and other technologies has revolutionized the way people communicate with each other and how people communicate in the professional world.

The main benefit technology serves in communication is that managers can get in touch with employees if they need something done when they are in different locations or outside of the scheduled work hours. Others make the argument that technology hinders the understanding of an employee when receiving tasks from the manager. Employees are not available to understand tasks over text message, phone call, or email as easily as they might absorb information in a face-to-face meeting.

While often overlooked, effective communication remains a strong trait to possess as a manager/leader. Managers need to be adept at one-to-one meetings, group meetings, and excel at online communication, such as messenger services, social media, video conferencing, and email. With effective communication, business deals get done faster and more efficiently. Most of the time, effective communication eliminates or compromises any with all parties involved, leaving everyone satisfied with the outcome.

In order to ensure that Gen Z doesn't repeat the same mistakes that plagued a lot of the previous generation's managers, we asked several Stevens Institute of Technology students to give their thoughts on how they would want their managers to communicate with them.

One student stated they wanted to first make sure that their manager was at least interested in what they were saying, elaborating that the manager's body language is crucial. Specifically, the student gave an example of when, in a one-on-one meeting with a manager, the manager shows that he or she is interested by sitting up straight rather than laying back in his or her chair, as well as maintaining eye contact at all times,"

"It is always appreciated when managers show they are listening by taking an extra second or two in order to process the information and then responding, rather than responding right away."

Gen Z Student, Age 21 - Stevens Institute Of Technology

Another student emphasized communication that is "clear, concise, and with purpose," and not rambling.

Employees often complain about how dull and monotonous their managers are. In other words, to the employees, it seems as if the managers are speaking because they just want to hear themselves talk, therefore likely reflecting the manager possessing an outsized ego.

Other resources managers should look to in order to better their communication skills is the Principles of Communication: 7C's. The 7C's are Correctness, Clarity, Concise, Concrete, Complete, Clear, Consideration, and Courteous (Toolshero, n.d.). Every gripe employees make about the way their managers communicate tend to stem from not adequately performing either one or multiple of the 7C's. Therefore, in order to master effective communication, Gen Z should use the 7C's as a guideline and master each component of the 7C's.

In the past, managers had to travel from branch to branch of a company to perform business assessments, meetings, and deals. With the introduction of video conferencing, business deals and meetings are made easier. Instead of flying over for every single meeting, companies can communicate with their businesses in other parts of the world with the only variable being sorting out the time difference. But while technology makes communication for managers more practical, managers still need to possess effective communication skills. Gen Z managers expect the majority of their meetings and conversations to include some sort of technology, whether it's via video conference or even through a simple text message. Gen Z managers know how important a role technology plays not only in today's world, but in the future as well.

Due to growth in technology, many more channels of communication have emerged. Our world is much different now due to new technologies, allowing for people to work without an office, nor even any office hours. Our communication in the workplace compared to previous years is undeniably different, as technology has affected the way everybody is keeping up with each other. Our Gen Z is so different that a manager can be communicating to hundreds of people over a screen, even if the manager is thousands of miles away. The more effort our generation puts into technology, the more we will be able to communicate with others.

Communication in the workplace is about getting to know employees, understanding what the plan is at all times, and executing the plan properly and on the same page as everybody else. Communication is essential to success in the business world, considering that if workers aren't talking to one another, there will be errors. Being able to understand the process and know the particular role a person has is crucial to keeping a business alive and to helping it thrive.

Gen Z must use every resource in the business world for success, and as society continues to grow and change, the workplace must as well. As the workplace changes, physical offices may not be nearly as common, meaning communication through technology will be even more important. New web browsing capabilities and faster file transfer software will make working at home much easier, in which communication with other co-workers and partners will be reliant on technology. Gen Z is ready to be working in teams, as working together on projects will be helpful, and Gen Z will be able to use their communication skills in order to get everything done. Gen Z also received the highest score on the UCLA loneliness scale (Berger, 2018), and although that may make employers worrisome about hiring people to work with one another.

One 19-year-old young student talked about how he feels that Gen Z will be very successful when put into teams or groups. The student said that when he is put into a group work environment, he will do a great job because of all the practice he has received from his many years in school, working on team projects with others.

Overall, effective communication is one of the most important skills to have as a leader in the business world. Therefore, it is imperative Gen Z master this skill—both online and face-to-face—in order to succeed. Gen Z have already proven they can adapt to the latest technology almost instantly. One of the critical turning points for Gen Z will be effectively communicating through technology in a professional way. The erratic rate at which technology is growing may concern people, but Gen Z is ready on the doorstep to alleviate those concerns.

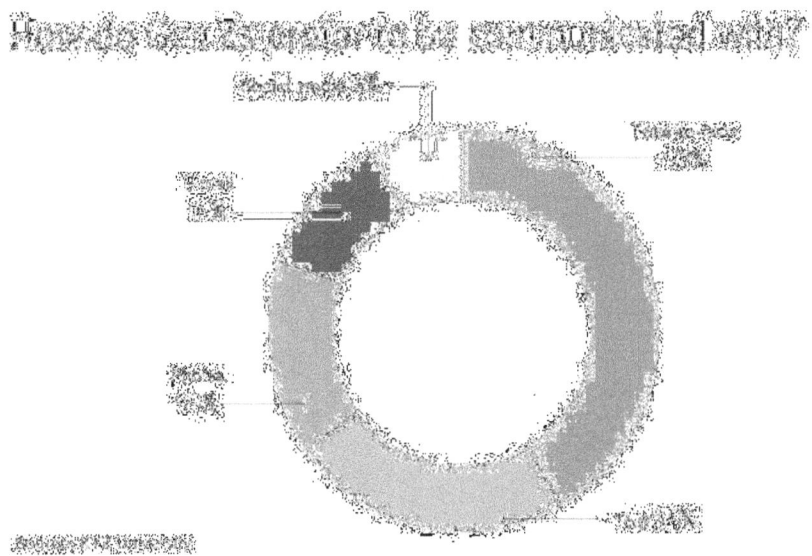

https://www.shrm.org/hr-today/news/hr-magazine/1118/pages/a-16-year-old-explains-10-things-you-need-to-know-about-generation-z.aspx

CHAPTER REFERENCES

Berger, S. (2018). Gen Z is the loneliest generation, survey reveals, but working can help. Retrieved May 4, 2019 from https://www.cnbc.com/2018/05/02/cigna-study-loneliness-is-an-epidemic-gen-z-is-the-worst-off.html

Hughes, J. (2018). Communicating with Generation Z. Everything You Need to Know. Retrieved May 4, 2019 from https://www.keystoneacademic.com/news/communicating-with-generation-z-everything-you-need-to-know

Lipman, V. (2015). The Type B Manager: Leading Successfully in a Type A World. New York: Prentice Hall Press

May, R. (n.d.). Brainy Quotes. Retrieved May 3, 2019 from https://www.brainyquote.com/quotes/rollo_may_389414

Russo, E. (n.d.). What's My Communication Style. Retrieved May 3, 2019 from http://www.hrdqstore.com/assets/downloadables/wmcs-infographic.pdf

Toolshero, (n.d.). 7Cs of Effective Communication. Retrieved May 5, 2019 from https://www.toolshero.com/communication-skills/7cs-of-effective-communication/

GEN Z AUTHORS

ANTHONY LANZA

Anthony is currently a freshman at Stevens Institute of Technology and he is majoring in Business & Technology with concentrations in the fields of Information Systems and Finance. Anthony is a part of Generation Z and he is excited to take part in the workforce using the principles learned through his first year of college. He believes his research is vital in the topic of managers being effective communicators.

JOSEPH SCHNEIDER

Joseph is currently a freshman at Stevens Institutes of Technology and is majoring in Business & Technology. Joseph is a part of Generation Z, and is very excited to use his newfound knowledge gained during his first year of college in order to succeed in the workforce. He believes his research is very important in the aspects of managerial communications.

JAISAL SHAH

Jaisal is currently a freshman attending Stevens Institute Of Technology, majoring in Business & Technology, with plans to minor in Quantitative Finance and/or Information Technology. Jaisal is part of Generation Z, and looks forward to use his skills learned during his first year of college in the business world in order to succeed in the workforce. He believes his research is of the utmost importance in terms of communication at the managerial level.

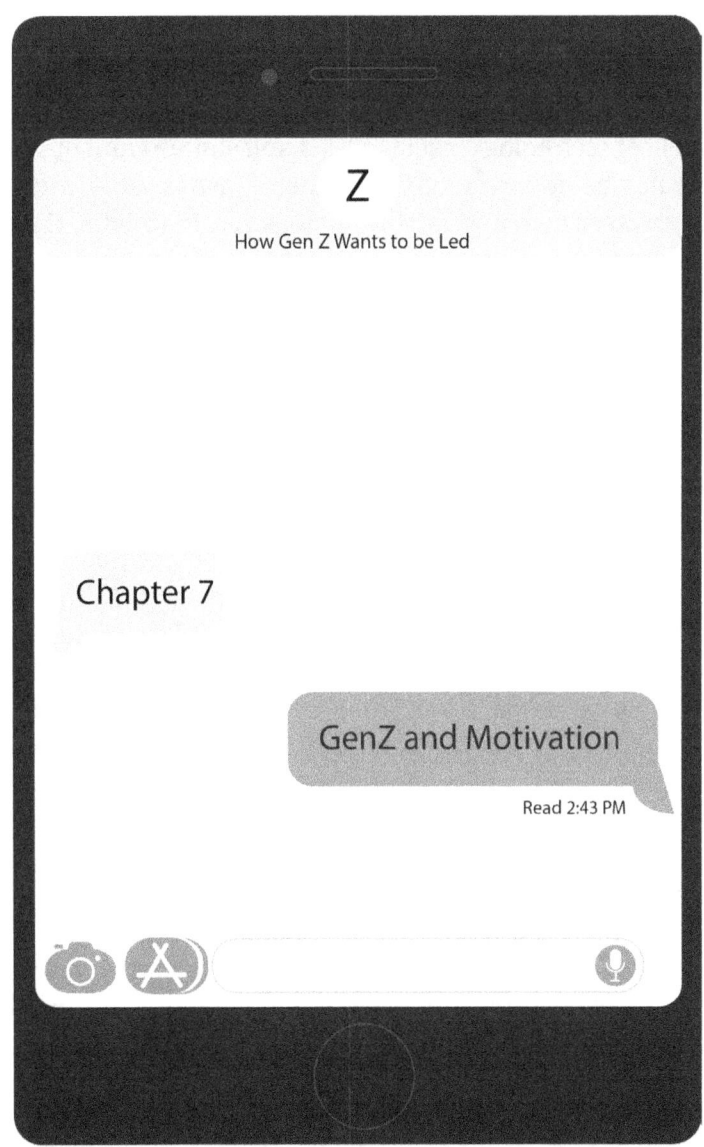

Z

How Gen Z Wants to be Led

Chapter 7

GenZ and Motivation

Read 2:43 PM

"The best way to motivate us is to understand us."

Gen Z, Age 21

Because of technology, social media and simple word of mouth, Gen Z has been portrayed in distinctive ways, often times by what excites them and, furthermore, what motivates them. In this chapter, we will examine a combination of behaviors in the past revealing particular values, coupled with observations on the generation's current state, to assess what motivates Gen Z.

As has been previously stated, Gen Z is the most "racially and ethnically diverse generation" currently in the United States (Fry & Parker, 2018). Their upbringing has enabled them to become more tolerant and accepting of others who are different than them. This generation possesses competitive qualities and entrepreneurial abilities, which empower them to be constantly thinking of new creative solutions. These individuals are ones with strong opinions; they want to be heard and want to act now to create a better environment. By understanding this generation and what motivates them, managers will be gaining a valuable and marketable skill.

Being raised in an era of 9/11, where safety became out of the question, and then a Great Recession, political conflicts, gun control and school terrorism, and global warming, Gen Z has become a generation that cares, a generation that is constantly stressed and overwhelmed with too many problems and not a clear way of solving them. This generation grew up in a world where economic pressure was applied during their childhood years, when their families lost their jobs and struggled to have ends meet. In addition to seeing their parents jobless, some may have lost savings for college tuition, which resulted in a realization to heavily value savings, owning property, and working hard to make a comfortable living. The previous generation, Millennials, came of age in a stable, growing economy with minor setbacks, making them far more optimistic about what's ahead of them than what Gen Z has experienced. Millennials wanted to give their lives more meaning while focusing on experiences and travel, leisure, work/life balance, etc.; they focus more on self-fulfillment and passion throughout their work. One such millennial working at Columbia Bank of New Jersey confirms this side of the argument:

"I am a huge advocate of work/life integration. It is best for me when my job is not demanding after hours or if I don't have to work late everyday. This is a big one for me because I enjoy working out after work. When I feel like I have time to myself in my personal life, then I am able to handle stress at work better."

In contrast, Gen Z differs from this perspective, because their environment forced them to be more realistic and rational.

"[Gen Z] view the purpose of work in the context of their lives and what the end goal of working everyday will look like."

Gen Z Student, Age 21 - Rutgers Business School

Members of Gen Z have developed a passion for resolving and fighting conflicts in the world. One of the top motivators for them coming from their leaders is to understand and talk about things that they truly care about. If you come to them and show them that you care, and at the same time, treat them like adults instead of like kids, they will show you their creative side, because they are focused on making a difference.

"Gen Z is more determined to make social changes while still being secure. This idea of security and making money and not being average in life is what motivates us. I feel like a lot of

it comes from our parents, because for the most part, they've lived pretty average/comfortable lives, but Gen Z is hungrier for success, from what I see."

Gen Z Student, Age 18 – University of Maryland

Gen Zers' childhood years, along with issues they have seen in their families firsthand, motivates them to be vigorous and ambitious, but also down to earth. Gen Z supports the idea of giving your children more than you had, and they are starting by creating for themselves the world that they have want to live in and be a part of.

Remember how vigorously members of Gen Z fought to bring justice for the 17 students that were killed in the Parkland, Florida shooting in 2018. Without a doubt, they went out there as a group, ready to protest and make a change. That was a big revolution for this generation—they created the national school walkout to express their strong opinions about gun rights and a "March for Our Lives," where they protested and encouraged more people to vote to make a change. These protests that have been led by this generation support the fact that they are not so pleased with following directions as how to deal with certain problems; instead, they are eager to find a way to prevent that problem from occurring at all. That is how they (will) act in the workforce; they (will) dedicate their time and act with devotion and determination to solve these issues.

Going back to security and stability, this generation typically finds that academic and professional achievements are among the most important factors in their jobs. They work hard for status and recognition rather than just for paying their college loans or bills. This generation is often accused of not willing to stay in a firm long enough if they do not receive some kind of praise or recognition in a short period of time, but Gen Zers will stay at a job for longer as long as they get this step up. Employers have been seeing many Gen Z workers asking for a promotion after a year of working. In fact, according to a recent survey completed by InsideOut Development (2019) who asked 1,000 people ages ranging from 18 to 23, more than 75% of Gen Z members believe they should be promoted in their first year on the job. They are highly motivated by recognition and are constantly thinking of moving higher up the ladder.

The Rutgers business student, however, has a different opinion and breaks this perception. She says that most of her class-mates' hopes for their careers (including hers) are "stability and ability to grow in a company," and that she, personally, "prefers to stay with one company more long-term and have them give [her] the tools [she] needs to grow, develop, and reach the top position in that company."

"I can definitely see the implications of the 2008 recession in my own career path as well, being that I spent a lot of time re-searching companies before I applied to internships and jobs because I wanted to make sure it was a stable, forward-think-ing organization," she continues. "This is a big reason why I chose L'Oréal. They are an extremely innovative company and have in-house think tanks and employee competitions where the company will legitimately invest in their own employees' business ideas."

A 19-year-old student from Georgetown University, has a dif-ferent take. "What motivates Gen Z is the fact that everybody shits on us," she says. "So, at work, we try to counter that and prove them wrong. We react well in the workforce. No one caus-es problems."

Gen Z students are open to new ideas and teaching themselves new skills every day from the constant exposure to technology. They take courses to learn how to code, work in Excel and Pho-toshop, and get exposure to new subjects like finance or web development. Lynda, part of LinkedIn, is a massive open online course website that offers countless amounts of video courses that are taught by professionals in software, design, business, web development, photography and many other fields teaching skills necessary for life. Social media has also been used for expressing these strong opinions and orchestrating movements like the #EnoughisEnough movement about gun control or about getting their generation to vote.

Another 19-year-old, studying International Criminal Justice at John Jay College, expressed that she has "more people skills than [her] coworkers" who are usually older and are in GenX or beyond. "We are more determined to succeed in the workforce; we are more competitive. Social media plays a huge role and it makes us work to show off."

As she inferred, social media platforms are often used to display one's accomplishments, whether it is a new job, a leadership role, a new business, a new written book, a community service, or even new designer apparel. They are also used to get donations for a specific organization that benefit a lot of those in need. Things like these make Gen Z more eager to accomplish better things and, of course, to compete with other people.

While we are still talking about social media, let's take a look at LinkedIn. This social media platform is flooded with Gen Z students that are eager to expand their networks and promote their ideas, express their opinions and also impress employers with their profiles and eventually get a job. Gen Z wants to connect and network. They get motivated by other successful people and want to grow, so networking events would be something they would look forward to attend.

The Millennial at Columbia Bank mentioned earlier in this chapter stated that "relationship building is a big motivation for our interns. If we set up interns to interact or collaborate with others on a project, I can see them very passionate and excited about the work."

This feeling like "they belong when they build these strong social connections" plays a huge role in being motivated to rise and accelerate. Leaders that wish to make sure this generation is greatly motivated in their workforce should organize networking events with external connections, bring in speakers that will push their limits even higher and integrate them in the firm's culture. If networking means growing and expanding quickly, they will be more than happy to do it. On the other hand, Gen Z also spends more time virtually communicating with others than previous generations, and for them, it would not make a difference if they complete an assignment at 8 A.M. or 8 P.M., because they can easily complete most assignment online, from home. While other generations are extremely displeased with being contacted at later hours, Gen Z individuals tend to be available at more times of the day. This pattern leads to a blurring of the line between work and everyday life; this is yet another difference between Gen Z and Millennials. Because of this, Gen Z is most likely going to be asked to work more hours than ever, or to deal with the reality that their work day will not end when they exit the office doors.

Even in popular music, says the John Jay student, "What promotes all this success is the songs, especially rap and hip hop. All they're singing about now is money and luxury. On the other side of the spectrum, older songs were more centered towards bars, love and romance."

Competition, as mentioned before, is huge for this generation. You will find Gen Zers hustling to their fullest, trying to grow as early as possible and as quickly as possible. Being motivated for focused goals allows one to also work productively in order to achieve them.

A 19-year-old Stevens student commented saying that she is definitely "fueled, empowered and driven by this competition and the constant desire to be successful. A sense of pride is con tributed to it too, as we know we know what we are capable of, want the best we deserve and are less likely to settle."

This same trend of individuals fighting to reach the top is echoed by another 19-year-old student, from the University of South Carolina.

"Everyone around us is competitive when it comes to work and college," she says. "For that reason, we are all trying to keep up with each other and while college used to be somewhat more optional, nowadays it's more of a necessity."

Motivation for most Gen Z individuals may tend to be driven by personal incentives, whether it is to stay out of the college debt, to leave a good impression on leaders in companies, or to earn bonuses or higher pay for the work they do. Gen Z lies in between working to sustain themselves and their families, as well as the additional idea of doing something they generally enjoy putting work towards and growing. Besides being goal-oriented, they are organized, often creating a mental checklist of what truly is important, and this allows for this generation to move forward in a successfully focused and driven manner.

Giving Gen Z the power to create their own projects while they are at a company and contribute their own personal insights, ideas and value makes them feel desired and motivated to provide more for a company. This feeling of purpose is what drives individuals to contribute their best work and truly motivates them. Certain priorities and pre-set goals motivate this generation to work quicker, more efficiently, and with more passion. Individuals in this generation seem to be more motivated to go into the workforce when leaders respect their input and value what they can contribute.

As it seems so far, this generation is driven by certain ideals and desires ingrained in their minds that include providing for themselves and possibly a family as well. This is demonstrated when students at a young age are forced to decide what they feel they have to do for the rest of their lives. Many of them are torn between doing something they love that drives them to keep going because of the way it inspires them, and something that may not be as "enjoyable" and requires more schooling but is worth it because of the reputation, financial benefits and respect that certain titles will give individuals.

It is common for someone to truly be motivated by graphic designing, but because becoming a doctor will be a major advantage to them, they will find a middle ground and pursue the pathway of becoming a physician's assistant as a career while pursuing design as a hobby. Although pay is important to this generation, they will oftentimes find a way to merge what they enjoy doing, with something that will provide for them financially as well. These high expectations and ideals are stemmed from them valuing the work they put in.

"Gen Z has such high expectations going into the workforce that I believe is rooted from how they were raised and what society shaped them into thinking and desiring from bosses," said a mother of three Gen Z children.

Misconceptions about Gen Z can be dissuaded once their motivation based on priorities, competition and desire to learn for the future comes to light. Companies that interest Gen Z will hold features that are of a significant value to them, such as coworkers that encourage them to achieve their best, a driven, challenging work environment, and strong, transparent systems in place that allow them to attain a higher salary. As soon as the older generations and even this generation can recognize and acknowledge that in a workplace, we are already off to a better start than we were before.

Gen Z is motivated by social rewards, mentorship, and constant feedback. They also want to do meaningful work and be given responsibility. Like their predecessors, they also demand flexible schedules. Other ways to motivate this generation are through experiential rewards and badges such as those earned in gaming and opportunities for personal growth. They also expect structure, clear directions, and transparency (Rampton, n.d.).

The one thing an employer has to offer to **Gen Z** to become an Ideal Employer

(Strazzulla, 2017)

CHAPTER REFERENCES

Fry, R. & Parker, K. (2018). Early Benchmarks Show 'Post-Millennials' on Track to Be Most Diverse, Best-Educated Generation Yet. Retrieved May 3, 2019 from: https://www.pewsocialtrends.org/2018/11/15/early-benchmarks-show-post-millennials-on-track-to-be-most-diverse-best-educated-generation-yet/

InsideOut Development (2019). Coaching Any Generation: A Pocket Guide for Managers and Mentors. Retrieved May 3, 2019 from: https://resources.insideoutdev.com/slideshare-all-slideshows-2/coaching-any-generation

Rampton, J. (n.d.) Different Motivations for Different Generations of Workers: Boomers, Gen X, Millennials, and Gen Z. Retrieved May 2, 2019 from: https://www.inc.com/john-rampton/different-motivations-for-different-generations-of-workers-boomers-gen-x-millennials-gen-z.html

Strazzula, P. (2017). Employees From All Generations Want This One Thing From Employers Retrieved May 7, 2019 from: https://www.entrepreneur.com/article/292254

GEN Z AUTHORS

TINA AHUJA

Tina is currently a freshman at Stevens Institute of Technology, and she is majoring in Business and Technology with concentrations in Marketing and Information Systems with a minor in International Business. Tina is a member of Generation Z and is enthusiastic about discovering more about the business world and integrating fashion with her passion for working on projects. She believes that research and involvement is vital in her pursuit of project management employment opportunities as she grows knowledge and status in this particular career path.

MATTHEW GROSS

Matthew is currently a junior at Stevens Institute of Technology and he is majoring in Finance with a minor in Quantitative Finance. Matthew is excited for the start of his professional career and is eagerly awaiting joining the workforce. He has strong opinions about how his generation differs from previous ones and is curious about how this generation will change the workplace culture.

ANA MICEVSKA

Ana is currently a freshman in Accounting and Analytics, and she is minoring in Quantitative Finance. She is passionate about fashion, numbers, and is very competitive, supporting the facts given in this chapter about Gen Z. She is not afraid to use her voice to express her opinions and ideas and is looking forward to using her social skills and intellect in the financial world.

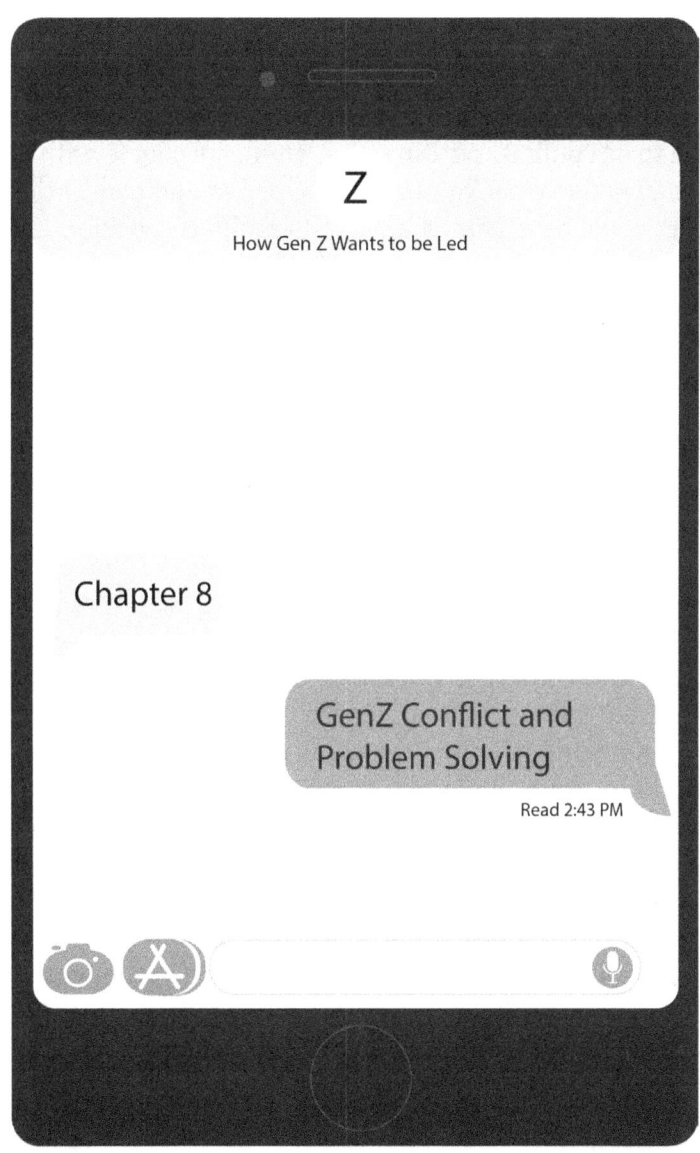

Z

How Gen Z Wants to be Led

Chapter 8

GenZ Conflict and Problem Solving

Read 2:43 PM

They believe profoundly in the efficacy of dialogue to solve
conflicts and improve the world.

(Francis & Hoefel , 2018)

In a world in which different roads often cross paths, there is
bound to be conflict. Within Gen Z, there are people with different perspectives, backgrounds, disciplines and conceptions. A
conflict could be a dispute amongst employees, leaders, a technical problem, or a challenge or friction between teammates.
Conflicts often arise from poor communication, personality dis-
agreements, or role disputes. A common mistake within communication is the assumption that the other party understands
the information being transferred. Within Gen Z, there is a belief that everyone thinks exactly alike. But everyone, regardless
of whatever similarities they might have, has a different way of
perceiving and understanding information.

One of the very valuable and delicate tasks that a leader manages is navigating conflict within the organization by following a fair but constructive process. To prevent conflict, leaders
should hold more discussions with those under them. However, not everyone is willing to speak up as many Gen-Zer's can
be afraid to argue their point in person. The discomfort of personal interaction can prevent someone from communicating
the problem to start with. Therefore, if a leader knows someone is not comfortable with speaking about an issue in a group
setting, they should bring up the dilemma in a more personal
atmosphere or discuss the conflict via email or a more private
means of communication. Gen Z is used to digital interaction.
Therefore, physical confrontation could be extremely difficult
for some Gen Zer's. Nonetheless, there is great significance behind physical interaction and communication. Reading body
language and signals can offer different input than virtual
communication. With various kinds of communication at their
disposal, Gen Zer's are more comfortable with transferring information.

To put it in perspective we collected a few opinions from Stevens Institute of Technology freshmen students and young entrepreneurs.

Question: *If you were a leader, how would you handle conflict between employees? Would you feel comfortable confronting them in person or discussing the problem over email?*

> Answer: *I handle conflict by manipulating a situation in which a mutual agreement can be reached by both parties easily. Usually, this will be resolved by email at first. If an email doesn't work, I will progress to a phone call or a meeting in-person as soon as possible to resolve the issue and make sure everyone is on the same page. In addition, if I want the individuals to collaborate as a team and bond, I will create a situation they don't know about that in which they need to work together for the best solution possible. (Brennan, 18-year-old CEO of Hoopswagg)*

Question: *As an employee, how do you think conflicts are best resolved?*

> Answer: *Gen Zers are very quick to assume things. If we all just took a step back and reevaluated the problem, we could maybe understand each other a little better, and think differently. If we are willing to accept different opinions, we could build a stronger empire together. (Nisha, 19-year-old student)*

Question: *"What is the best way to manage Gen Z employees, as a Gen Zer yourself?"*

> Answer: *"As a fellow Gen Zer, I've found the best way to manage Gen Z employees is how I work best. Under a performance-based system, where there are strong incentives based off of goals." (Jesse, 18-year-old CEO of Vyber Media)*

Question: *What do you believe causes the most conflict?*

> Answer: *Gen Zers aren't willing to accept someone else's ideas because of complexes. Some Gen Zers are very willing to accept other ideas, especially if they are good ideas, however, very often, Gen Zers don't want to follow someone else's idea. They believe that their idea is best. It is with this type of mentality, that Gen Zers cannot move forward and progress because they are stuck in their own system. (David, 18-year-old student)*

Gen Zers often struggle with communication, because they misinterpret the concept of "two ears, one mouth." Gen Zer's struggle with this in particular because of their reliance on having two eyes, and only their voice on social media. Given the reality that we're on the screen more than we are physically communicating, Gen Zer's are more likely to observe and complain through the phone rather than speak up about a problem in person. This ultimately causes conflict in an organization because of all the potential miscommunication or lack of trust that can arise. Whether the information that is being shared is an idea, an order, or a task, it is important that it is communicated correctly and clearly. Nothing successful was brought up by simply one individual. In order to create something big and bold, everyone needs to be invested. However, it is only with key and proper communication that groups of individuals are able to become teams.

Gen Zers are often afraid to share an opinion. With today's constantly rising standards, high competition and fear built from screen adaption, Gen Zers are more adverse than any prior generation to sticking to their beliefs against pushback from others. Given today's tasks and increase in challenging projects, the standard is set very high for pleasing other people and attracting an interested crowd. With today's fast paced culture and progress with technology, it is difficult to express everything that you want to say in one medium. This is why the feelings that Gen Zers have about things are constantly changing. With a very high standard in success and outcome, it can become very intimidating to stay true to what you believe while everyone around you thinks otherwise. Finally, attracting other people into liking your ideas causes people to overthink their own ideas, in an effort to please others. Without a concrete opinion, Gen Zers follow others blindly and switch between them in a frenzy. This causes conflict as visions and ideas begin to fade from fear and discomfort. If Gen Z can build the persistence and courage to speak up and solidify their thoughts, then as a generation we can have the power to withhold criticism, apply it and reconstruct the problem for the better.

Gen Zers suffer from an inability to distinguish between the physical and digital worlds in which they live. We can refer to this as the "Phigital" (Stillman & Stillman, 2017) world that Gen Zers inhabit. 91% of Gen Zer's report that a company's technological sophistication would influence their desire to work for that company. As true as this is, the dependence on technology has slowed Gen Z 's other cognitive skills such as critical problem solving and navigation. Orientation cognition is valuable because without orientation, people get lost in the process, disorganizing and disrupting operations.

Organizational culture is essential. However, companies that blend different backgrounds and generations can create more sustainable advantages. With different backgrounds and insight, people offer perspectives that channel different ideas and visions for the company. However, as beneficial as different minds are, they can cause problems. When people think differently, they can easily form quarrels with each other, leading to arguments. With different traditions, disciplines, ideas and mentalities, people are able to create an organizational culture that is diverse but meets criteria that everyone can relate to. People are more likely to be a part of something they are familiar with, rather than completely new. Therefore, an interesting organizational culture attracts more and different people.

Pleasing Gen Z is a matter of attributing fast results. If they don't receive what they want from one person, they look to obtain it from the next. This creates a problem, as Gen Zers can become disrespectful and lacking persistence. The truth is that you cannot please everyone. Despite being diligent workers on tasks, if it is not done a certain way for some Gen Zers, then it cannot be done at all. To solve this problem, leaders can initiate ways to link their employees and have them bond over particular things. Getting people to open their perspective is difficult, because not everyone thinks the same way. People often use the excuse that they're not used to something being done in a certain way. People need to understand that if they're in a shared environment, they must be willing to change their old habits. It was their decision to be where they are. If they do not feel they function well or contribute to the company, then they can find another place.

Despite trouble confronting the problem, Gen-Zers are known to be a part of the "do it yourself" generation. Since they are a very independent generation, they fear the collisions with other organizational and collaborative cultures catalyzed by other generations. It's difficult to translate the fast and constant tempo they are comfortable with to other generations. What was once their the older norm no longer exists, however that fact is difficult for some to grasp, and it can cause conflict.

A leader should always stick by having two ears and one mouth. No conflict can be solved if someone is not willing to listen more than speak. It takes two people to form an argument. A leader who is willing to solve conflicts should be able to acknowledge that there is one in the first place. When there is a problem in a firm, there should always be a rational explanation. Sometimes, people argue over miniscule things. Therefore, it is also the leader's job to properly discipline their employees. Arguments over irrational subjects should not cause conflicts or any dilemma in a firm to start with.

Among members of Gen Z, there is a constant urge for instant gratification. Given that everything is constantly moving at a fast pace, if it doesn't work the first time, they either move onto something else or give up. Persistence and tempers have lowered significantly. Nonetheless, there is also a very cautious weariness within Gen Z. Given the disciplines and upbringing amid the aftermath of 9/11, hacking, and other attacks, there is a new-found skepticism in their world outlook. Gen Zers are very aware of the scary reality of technology. They know that behind every screen is another monitor that is watching them and their activity. This prepares Gen Z for the technological problems that are a part of virtual reality.

Gen Zers are also entering into an age of customization. Gen Zers are used to everything that they use being tailored to their preferences and expect nothing less than their perfect vision for whatever product they are using. This makes it incredibly difficult to both create products for Gen Zers, as well as to work with them towards a goal that they may already have a plan for attaining themselves. This also extends to the kinds of jobs for which Gen Zers will be searching the market. 56% of Gen Zers want the ability to write their own job descriptions (Stillman & Stillman, 2017). This sense of entitlement and need for control over every facet of their life makes it very hard for Gen Zers to be satisfied. To solve this Gen Z problem, the generation as a whole must find equilibrium between their high standards and realistic expectations.

One of the most recognizable traits that come with members of Gen Z include their innate fear of "missing out" on something. This FOMO can be a tough emotion to cope with for many Gen Zers. The good news that comes from this is that Gen Zers will always be aware of the latest news and will always have access to strong social connections. Unfortunately, this also means that the worry that they will have about not moving fast enough will result in them always feeling as if they haven't done enough. By not feeling that they have done enough, Gen Z are at risk of carrying with them a lack of fulfillment.

Gen Zers are professionals when it comes to working within a shared economy. Whether it's through Uber, Airbnb, or everything in between, Gen Zers are very well acquainted with their roles as "Weconomists" (Stillman & Stillman, 2017). Gen Zer's push to break down internal and external silos through the power of these shared economies. This can be very beneficial in the sense that a shared economy allows for individuals to share expenses with each other and overall walk away with more cost-effective experiences as consumers. However, downsides do exist when Gen Zers place such a dependence on the sharing economy because this dependence can blind them to the risks that come along with it, which include the possibility of an invasion of privacy, the absence of security, and the lack of a guarantee of service.

Fearing independent nature will collide head-on with so many of the collaborative cultures that Millennials have fought for, people in Gen Z are less likely to follow in someone else's footsteps. Despite being a competitive generation that is motivated by others' successes, Gen Z are not as willing to listen to others. This causes conflict because, as a generation, they take so much pride in doing everything in a way that is unique to them and can sometimes overlook the value that comes with drawing inspiration from others.

Gen Zers have had it drilled into them through their parents that in life, there are winners and losers, with nothing in between. Gen Zers are a motivated group, with 72% of them saying that they are competitive with people who are doing the same job as them (Stillman & Stillman, 2017).

The conflict that might arise for Gen Z stems in large part from their stubbornness and unwillingness to change. Simultaneously, they are a generation that is extremely independent from each other but dependent on technology. Suboptimal communication is ultimately what leads to conflicts. However, to solve the problem, Gen Z should be more willing to express themselves and listen to what others have to say. It is with a different but open perspective that we can find the match of that "good idea."

The search for the truth is at the root of all Generation Z's behavior.

'Undefined ID'	'Communaholic'	'Dialoguer'	Realistic
"Don't define yourself in only one way"	"Be radically inclusive"	"Have fewer confrontations and more dialogue"	"Live life pragmatically"

Expressing individual truth	Connecting through different truths	Understanding different truths	Unveiling the truth behind all things

McKinsey&Company

https://www.mckinsey.com/industries/consumer-packaged-goods/our-insights/true-gen-generation-z-and-its-implications-for-companies

CHAPTER REFERENCES

Francis, T. & Hoefel, F. (2018), "True Gen: Generations Z and its implications for companies. Retrieved May 2, 2019 from https://www.mckinsey. com/industries/consumer-packaged-goods/our-insights/true-gen-generation-z-and-its-implications-for-companies

Jenkins, Ryan. "How Generation Z Will Transform the Future Workplace." Inc.com, Inc., 15 Jan. 2019, www.inc.com/ryan-jenkins/the-2019-workplace-7-ways-generation-z-will-shape-it.html.

Stillman, David, and Jonah Stillman (2017). "Gen Z @ Work: How the Next Generation Is Transforming the Workplace." Amazon, Amazon. www.amazon. com/Gen-Work-Generation-Transforming-Workplace/dp/0062475444.

GEN Z AUTHORS

NATHAN BAWDUNIAK
Stevens Institute of Technology class of 2022 Business and Technology Major with Minor in Quantitative Finance. Nathan believes that identifying ways of managing Generation Z is essential. As a member of Gen Z this research will help him excel in his professional life.

JESSE KAY
Jesse is currently a freshman at Stevens Institute of Technology and he is majoring in Marketing at the business school. Jesse is a member of Gen Z and owns his own digital marketing agency, Vyber Media which works with brands on better connecting with Gen Z through digital and social media marketing. He knows these insights are incredibly valuable and will help the next generation of leaders properly employ Gen Z.

MARIJA STOJKOSKA
Marija is currently a freshman at Stevens Institute of Technology and she is majoring in Business and Technology. Marija is a member of Generation Z. She is excited to be able to represent her generation and elaborate on the tactics she has picked up on regarding the technology and the workforce, as she explains in part of this documentation. She believes that Generation Z is the future that will bring new connections between technology and people together.

JOHN HARTOFILIS
John is currently a Freshman at Stevens Institute of Technology in the Class of 2022. He is Majoring in Business and Technology with Concentrations in Management and Information Systems, and a minor in Economics. John is a member of Generation Z and is excited about what the future holds for Generation Z. John is the Assistant Coach for the Xavier High School Freshman Basketball Team as well as the Media Director for Super League Athletic Academy. John believes that his involve-

ment in this project will allow him to further pursue possible employment in these fields.

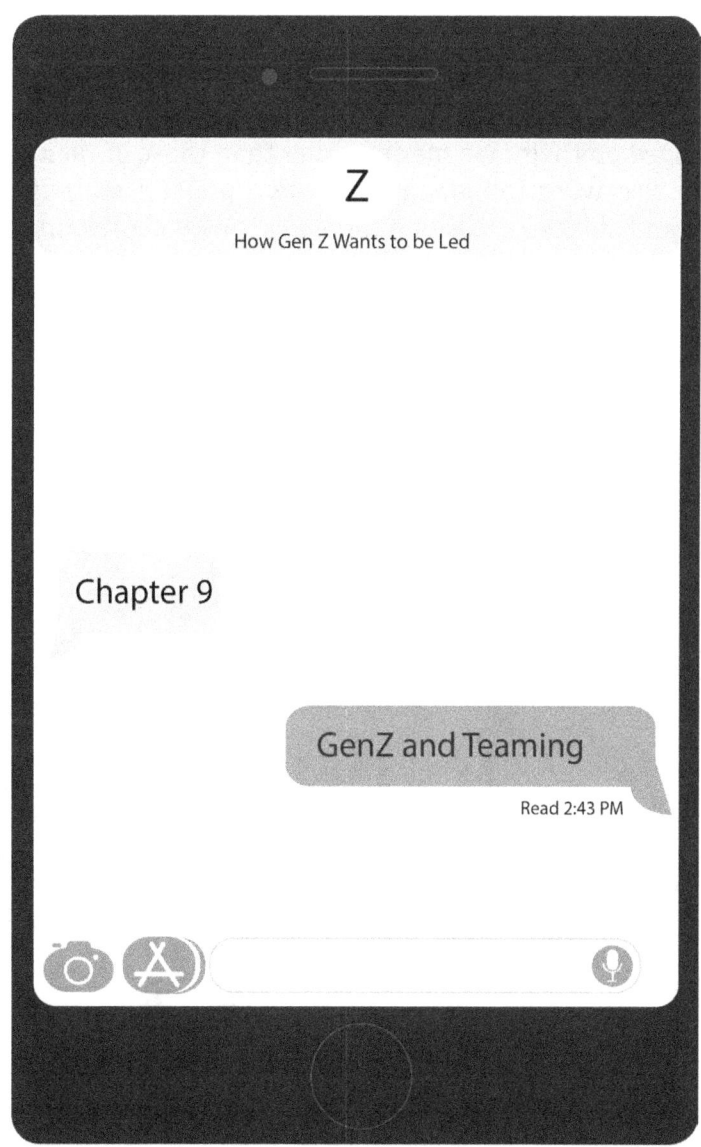

Z

How Gen Z Wants to be Led

Chapter 9

GenZ and Teaming

Read 2:43 PM

As a cohort, millennials are said to be collaborative and team-work oriented. They want to work in an environment where inclusion is a priority, and where everybody works together to advance goals. Gen Z, on the other hand, is said to be defined by its competitiveness. They want to work on their own and be judged on their own merits rather than those of their team. Many also want to manage their own projects so that their skills and abilities can shine through. They do not want to depend on other people to get their work done.
(Patel, 2017)

https://www.mediavillage.com/article/welcoming-gen-z-be-inclusive-or-youll-be-irrelevant/

GENERATION Z
VS
MILLENNIALS

INDIVIDUAL

Generation Z:
Individual performance
and growth

TEAM

Millennials:
Work in teams
for greater whole

MONEY

Prefer structure &
job security;
motivated by money

PURPOSE

Motivated by
bigger purpose

PRIVACY

Prefer working alone
in their own
workplace

OPEN

Enjoy working in
large, open
areas

COMMONALITY: DIGITAL NATIVES

Both generation z and millennials
are digital natives who stuggle
to stay on task.

Infographic brought to you by **office**

https://www.iofficecorp.com/blog/move-over-millennials-generation-z-is-coming-for-the-workplace

Working as part of a team is a crucial skill to have when entering the workforce. If someone cannot work well with others and contribute to a team effort, their career may not last long. Working in a team is most likely not a new concept to Gen Zers entering the workforce. Some people thrive in this type of working environment, while some would rather work individually. In this chapter, the way Gen Z views working in a team is discussed as well as what types of teams and experiences they can expect to see in their working careers.

Being a part of a team is something that nearly every person experiences at some point in their life. Whether the team was a Little League baseball team or a high school debate team, the collaborative elements that existed on those teams is reaching further in organizations of all types and sizes. As they come into the workforce, Gen Zers will most likely work in teams on an everyday basis, and how they work in a team can affect the success of their career.

Trying to find the secret to assembling perfect teams that collaborate and work well together is something that companies have been pursuing for generations. Teams transform the workplace with open and collaborative discussion as well as clear communication of expectations and understanding. Gen Z will impact how successful these teams will really be as they flock into the workforce and join them.

Gen Z can bring a lot into the workplace while working in a team, because they bring new perspectives that the previous generations might not have. Members of previous generations working in a team with Gen Zers can spark new ideas and solutions to problems that companies and businesses might face when trying to grow or evolve. The previous generations bring experience to the table, because they have been around in the world for a longer period of time and have likely gone through changes in the business before. Gen Z, on the other hand, has the experience with social media and all the new technology that has grown into today's world.

Technology is a big part of everybody's daily life and Gen Z were placed right into this world of expanding technology and smart devices. In a team, they bring this experience and knowledge to the table and are able to leverage the technology that they have used their whole lives to help solve problems. Gen Z has been shown to bring certain qualities to a team that older generations might not be able to bring. First, they bring the concept of planning ahead to the workforce. Previous generations like Baby Boomers and Generation X are older than everyone else in the workforce and their first priority might not be to plan ahead with their business, but it is necessary to look at the future of your business so you have goals and deadlines to reach in order to be successful.

Gen Z also embraces remote working, which is working together in a team through technology and not always through in-person contact. This can allow teams to conquer problems more quickly, saving time instead of having to always meet up at work or a shared location. This can be beneficial to a team because it also allows people to be make time to work from home and not have to devote part of their daily schedule to a commute.

Even though it is not their first preference, most members of Gen Z know how to work well within teams and improve whatever workplace environment they are in. A large concern among many members of Gen Z today is that there will be an unreliable group member that does not get their work done or forces others on the team to do it for them.

"I do like working teams or groups when everyone works together," a 19-year-old student at Sacred Heart University said. "Sometimes it is hard to rely on other people with important matters."

Another student, from Stevens Institute of Technology, said, "In general, I'm not a fan, because lots of 'group work' ends up being individual work."

These concerns of Gen Z can be fixed by ensuring that the team culture is well developed and conducive to a productive environment.

It is interesting to see that most of the reasoning of why Gen Z members do not enjoy working in groups is due to lack of trust that others will properly do their work. Apart from that, they seem to have few inhibitions about working collaboratively.

An 18-year-old student from Stevens said it "depends on my team members. If they are smart and willing to do work, then group work is great. If they are incompetent, then I would rather work by myself."

Most of Gen Z has not entered the workforce yet so most of the teamwork they have participated in at this point has probably only been either a group project in school or a team sport. Even though young adults may not have had the best experiences in working in teams, it is a crucial learning experience and precursor to many occupations, and they will need to find a way to enjoy working in a group or team.

In order to evenly distribute the workload in a team, roles and responsibilities need to be given to the best candidate. The team also needs to have a common goal they are working towards, this way, the team members can be motivated to reach that goal and work in collaboration. There are many benefits to working in a team as well, such as combining the skills and strengths of multiple people and increasing the employee morale in the company.

A 19-year-old student from New York University said, "I like working in a team because you get to share ideas and work out various possible solutions to problems."

An 18-year-old student from Boston College shared a similar viewpoint, saying, "I love working in a group because collaborating produces better ideas."

The idea of sharing ideas is a very beneficial factor for working in a team. When more people work together to either pitch an idea or solve a problem, the chances of having a successful outcome increase.

"I feel that working in a group can be very beneficial if you have a strong leader who can designate well and group members who are willing and able to cooperate with each other," said a 19-year-old student at Stevens.

This person brings up a valid point that a strong leader can help to improve the group experience when working in a team, whether that leader is a coach, a manager, or simply someone appointed to help guide all the members toward their common goal. Another factor brought up is that the members work together. In order for a group to be efficient and effective, all members need to work in unison.

If one person in the group is slacking, the whole group's efforts can be ruined. As Gen Z enters the workforce, they need to be prepared to be a reliable group member and to know their responsibilities and do them.

A 20-year-old student at James Madison University said, "I enjoy working in a team or on a group as long as all members are determined and capable of pulling their own weight."

It is important for Gen Z to know that no matter how small their role in the group may be, they have people relying on them to get the work done.

Sometimes, teams can include members from outside of a company as well, which makes it important for Gen Z to be able to communicate properly with people they are not necessarily familiar with. A self-managed team is something Gen Z will also see in the workforce and need to be prepared for as well. With this type of team, the members of a group must be working collaboratively because they are responsible for a big task. Another common type of team is a cross-functional team. In a cross-functional team, there are members from all different departments of a company working towards that one common goal. Members could include employees from finance, IT, marketing, or human resources. Gen Z will have to be aware of these teams and be able to work together with people from different sides of the company.

In today's climate, a virtual team may be the most common form of team that Gen Z will encounter. With the help of technology such as email, phone calls, and video conferencing, people are able to work with others from across the globe. In these types of teams, there may be some barriers such as time difference, language, culture, or even miss communication. Gen Z will have to work through these barriers as the work culture becomes more and more virtual and technology reliant. They will need to be aware of these in order to work smoothly and effectively in a team. If that means taking a call late at night in order to reach members in a different country, Gen Z must adjust to that in order to work with their team.

A team also cannot be forced out of anywhere. There are five important stages that Gen Z should be aware of in the process of team development that are highlighted in the "Team Development Model" created by educational psychologist Bruce Tuckman (LumenLearning, n.d.). The five stages are forming, storming, norming, performing, and adjourning. Forming is the beginning stage of team development, when everyone is trying to figure out where they belong (LumenLearning, n.d.). A team leader may be discussed at this time, as people are looking for authority and direction. The next stage is storming, in which a common goal is discussed and team members get to know one another better. This is a very crucial stage in team development and can also be very challenging for teams to get through, because the conflict between team members is very common during this stage (LumenLearning, n.d.).

The third stage in team development is norming. In this stage, roles and responsibilities are discussed and collaboration between team members is increased (LumenLearning, n.d.). This stage also involves increased team performance as well, since all members should be working toward their common goal in unison. The fourth stage is performing, at which point the team's work should be running smoothly and effectively (LumenLearning, n.d.). The team should be aware of what their roles are and the team itself should have a secure foundation. The last stage in team development is adjourning (LumenLearning, n.d.). In this final stage, the last piece of the puzzle is usually put together. Team members will finish up their tasks at hand and make sure the goal for the team was met.

With the work that comes from teams being better than it had been coming from individuals, there have even been experiments with hiring groups to do jobs instead of single workers. The possibility to gain the expertise of a whole team of people who have worked together in the past and have a strong sense of what it means to work with a team is something very exciting.

A 19-year-old student from the College of Charleston said, "I enjoy working in a team or group when I am working with people I can rely on and am comfortable with."

Teaming across generations doesn't always go smoothly, and some disagreement can arise from working with this new generation. Even though Gen Z can bring new ideas to the team using their modern knowledge, previous generations might not always see things the same way. For example, Baby Boomers and Generation X might prefer to do things in person and solve their issues in person, instead of handling things digitally. A Gen Z person, however, might like the idea of solving problems digitally or doing things more online than in person.

Although it may seem like a simple concept, working in a team is something that not everyone may enjoy. There are many different aspects that contribute to whether or not the team will be successful. As Gen Z continues to enter the workforce they will experience new ways of working in a team such as those discussed in this chapter. If they can remember some of the key elements that makes any team successful, even from when they were a child, Gen Z can make their mark on the workforce as a hardworking, unique and intelligent generation.

HOW GEN Z WORK WITH OTHER GENERATIONS

THEY WOULD PREFER COMMUNICATING WITH **CO-WORKERS** AND MANAGERS **IN PERSON** RATHER THAN BY **EMAIL OR BY PHONE**

64% OF GEN Z PREFER TO WORK IN A **SMALL** TEAM WITHIN AN **OFFICE** SETTING

72% OF GEN Z WORKERS FEEL **COMPETITIVE** WITH PEOPLE DOING THE SAME JOB

GEN Z WANTS CREDIT FOR THEIR WORK, AND EXPECTS TO BE REWARDED FOR THEIR **INDIVIDUAL ACHIEVEMENTS** THEY ARE HAPPIER **WORKING ALONE** THAN ALWAYS AS PART OF A GROUP

64%

https://www.google.com/search?client=firefox-b-1-d&biw=1500&bih=861&tbm=isch&sa=1&ei=fF-HUXP7JluOl_QbepLnQDw&q=gen+z+and+attitudes+about+teams+at+work&oq=gen+z+and+atti-tudes+about+teams+at+work&gs_l=img.3...152946.165274..166033...7.0..0.350.2367.32j2j0j1......1....1..gws-wiz-img.6uvoP8_4E9U#imgrc=1oYR8GkHbNrCaM:

CHAPTER REFERENCES

Lumen Learning, (n.d.). The Five Stages of Team Development. Retrieved May 8, 2019 from: https://courses.lumenlearning.com/suny-principlesmanagement/chapter/reading-the-five-stages-of-team-development/

Patel, D. (2017). 8 Ways Generation Z Will Differ From Millennials In The Workplace. Retrieved May 9, 2019 from: https://www.forbes.com/sites/deeppatel/2017/09/21/8-ways-generation-z-will-differ-from-millennials-in-the-workplace/#6ed742d676e5

GEN Z CO-AUTHORS

Kristyn Norkus - Kristyn is a sophomore at Stevens Institute of Technology and she is a Business and technology major with concentrations in Marketing and Information Systems. As a member of Generation Z and as someone who is entering the workforce soon, Kristyn believes that having this knowledge and research about Gen Z will benefit her greatly for her future.

Brendan Sullivan - Brendan is a freshman at Stevens Institute of Technology and he is a Finance major. Brendan believes that the information that has been researched about the impact of Gen Z in the workforce will benefit him as he is preparing to enter the workforce in the near future.

Corinne Dougherty - Corinne is a freshman at Stevens Institute of Technology and a Business and technology major. As someone who is eager to join the workforce in the coming years, Corinne finds this information to be some of the most important you could learn in your college years.

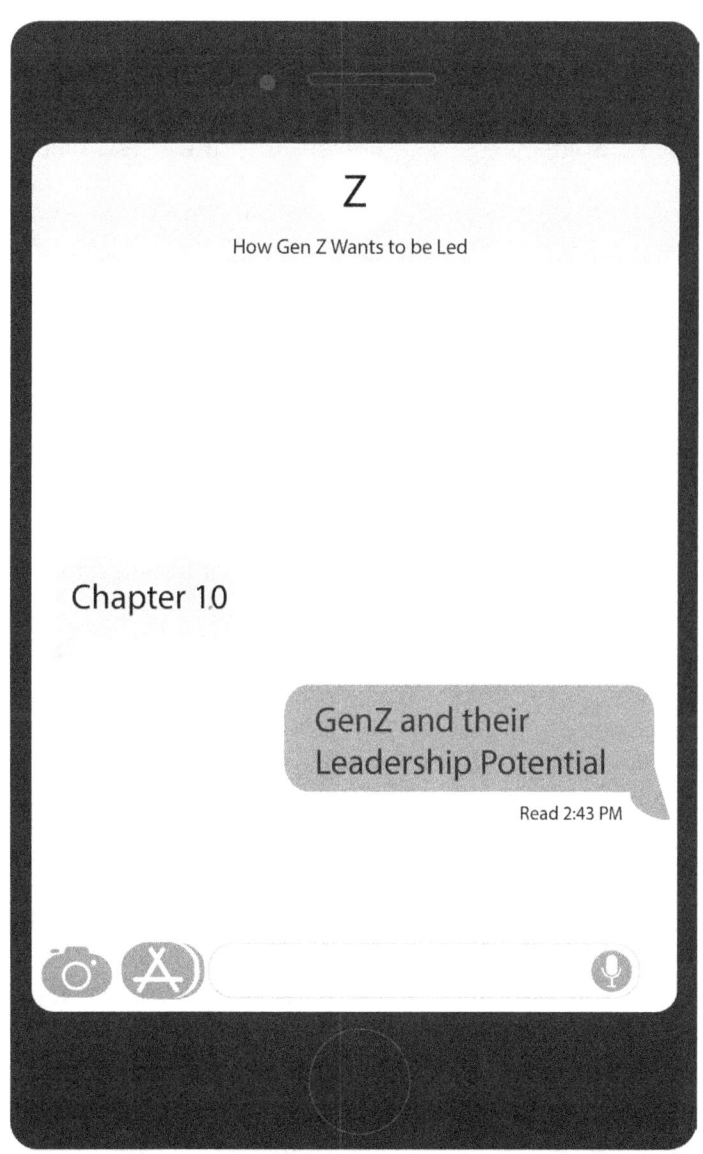

Z

How Gen Z Wants to be Led

Chapter 10

GenZ and their
Leadership Potential

Read 2:43 PM

"Over time, leadership potential has been broken down to a science. We know most of the things that make a great leader, but in the future, that last bit we don't know is going to be vital because of how quickly business evolves."

Gen Z Student, Age 21 – Stevens Institute of Technology

A natural part of a person's career is a promotion and the increased level of responsibility associated with it. Good performance over an extended period of time will result in a person being rewarded with promotions, in most cases. Of the people that will be promoted in their careers, few are able to transition into leadership positions. While most companies evaluate a person's leadership potential differently, this chapter will look to discuss, generally, how leadership potential is assessed, where Gen Z falls in the assessment and whether the assessment should be reconsidered.

What is Leadership Potential?

"Leadership potential is the potential a person has to be a leader. That's not too helpful, but it's hard to define"
Gen Z, Age 21, Student – Stevens Institute of Technology

In layman's terms, explaining what leadership potential is can be very difficult and often provides an answer that isn't particularly helpful. Yet, everyone has their own understanding of what leadership potential is. Leadership potential is a range of abilities and traits that are related to success as a leader. There is no concrete list, but there are some traits that are commonly looked for regardless of the company.

Characteristics like aspiration, ability and drive are commonly found in successful leaders and should be emulated by others. Aspiration is defined as the drive for a goal, results or advancement in general is very important for assessing leadership potential, as an aspiring leader is a non-complacent leader.

Understanding a person's aspirations provides insights into what drives them, which is important information when considering a potential leader. Similar to aspiration, a person's level of engagement is important to evaluate as it represents that person's commitment to their work. The last characteristic, and likely the most commonly looked for, is a person's ability. While there is some room for interpretation when it comes to ability depending on where a subject is in his or her career and what level of leadership opportunity they are being considered for, having the ability to do a job is always beneficial. Having these three characteristics won't guarantee that one will have a high potential to be a leader, as there are many factors outside of your control at work, but it certainly will increase their chances (Bridgespan Group (n.d.).

How is leadership potential assessed?

While the assessment for leadership potential varies from company to company, there is a typical pattern that is followed. Leadership potential is typically determined by comparing a person's performance relative to their potential. The simplest form of evaluating the relationship between these two is in the 9-box method (Mccarthy, 2018), a graphical representation of which can be found below.

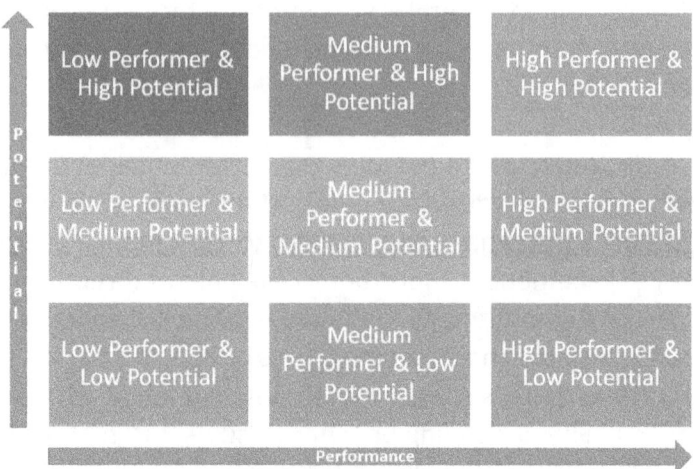

In the 9-box method, performance and potential are ranked into 3 categories: low, medium and high. Based on how a person is evaluated, they will fall into one of the 9 boxes shown above. Of the two factors, performance is easier to assess and can be done with relatively minimal error and bias. Potential is assessed by evaluating a person's personality and cognitive traits. Personality traits are those that are interpersonal results and emotional versatility whereas cognitive traits are those related to how a person learns new concepts and solves problems. Given the way technology has progressed, cognitive traits can be evaluated through tests. Companies value cognitive prowess highly as many require applicants to complete cognitive tests as part of the recruiting process. Personality traits are harder to determine as they can only be examined through actual interaction (Mccarthy, 2018).

"Personality traits are more important when evaluating person's leadership potential. You can improve your cognitive traits, but not so much your personality. Good cognitive traits can be used to get the solution, but personality traits allow you to actually execute."

Gen Z Student, Age 20 – Stevens Institute of Technology

Will this assessment need to change?

"No, I feel that leadership is a skill derived from one's emotional intelligence combined with their skill in their respective subject."

Gen Z Student, Age 22 – Stevens Institute of Technology

Like many topics related to leadership, it's not a simple black and white answer. The 9-box method seems simple enough and captures the two things most important for assessing one's capacity for leadership: performance and potential. The components and the weightings associated with them should be reevaluated to reflect the current work environment. Performance assessments are generally well regarded in this area and can remain the same as they typically have little bias and error. Potential assessments should include new and re-weighted factors to reflect the current, diverse work environment.

Communication, emotional intelligence and open mindedness should either be included or weighted higher, as the current workforce consists of various ages, races and geographical regions. For a leader, the ability to communicate is very important, as you will spend most of your career communicating your ideas to others. Having good communication skills allows for more efficient work and allows for your followers to understand your vision better. High emotional intelligence is important as well, because we exist in a world that is very results-driven. Due to the demand for results, leaders are under constant pressure to keep improving. Regardless of how technically capable a leader may be, without emotional intelligence they will not be able to execute their vision. Leadership potential should also look at whether a person is open minded and flexible. Technology and the workforce are changing too rapidly for leaders to remain stagnant and keep a narrow mindsight. While there are countless other things to look for in leadership potential, these are both the more important ones, but also the most fathomable to come by.

Where does Gen Z fall in this assessment?

"With the technology present in our day and age, I feel that our generation has the resources to be more successful because our ideas are now interconnected due to the internet."

Gen Z Student, Age 19 - Stevens Institute of Technology

Gen Z has a completely different mind-set than other generations in that they are capable of being both independent and dependent at the same time. Gen Z are more dependent than generations before the Millennials but more independent than Millennials, themselves.

As we said previously, a leader needs to have essential qualities such as communication. It is impossible to have good results without good communication between a manager and his employees, regardless of age. Indeed, the manager's function is to communicate the ambitions of the company. Communication is also important for the manager in terms of the wellbeing of the employees. One of the manager's tasks is to look over the employee's satisfaction, in case he or she might work harder if he feels he has recognition in his work. A leader coming from Gen Z will have this quality of communicating with the employee. Gen Z leaders are born in a time where relationships and money are not all that they are working for. They work more for satisfaction than for other reasons.

"Based on the classes and the opportunities I've seized at Stevens; I am prepared for the workforce and to express my leadership abilities. The most valuable lessons I have learned, have been outside of the classroom when traveling, working

retail and have been working with professor's advice."

Gen Z Student, Age 20 - Stevens Institute of Technology

In addition, Gen Z is prepared by studies to work very early: colleges in general are trying to teach students everything they need to start working efficiently when they graduate. It is valuable for companies to hire people that are highly qualified but also ones who are able to get started without needing an explanation on how everything works. Those studies include classes about leadership. It is a huge advantage as those classes did not exist in previous generations. Gen Z workers will not have to learn on the field and will save valuable time. Having young leaders in company could be a precious advantage as they have a different vision of how to lead a company than old leaders.

Because of the conditions in which they are living in (new technologies, moving countries, travelling, talking multiple languages) members of Gen Z are well trained to adapt, overcome, and succeed in most any type of circumstances. Adapting fast is a game changer in our world, and adaptability and flexibility are qualities that should be useful while being a leader.

In the diagram shown in above we could grade Gen Z potential after enumerating all the skills they have. The ranking they have should be between high and medium as they have obvious qualities to succeed, but they are just unpolished and need to be worked on.

How does our generation compare to previous generations?

"There is a large gap in levels of leadership among people in our generation, because a lot of people in our generation have not been exposed to as many situations that require leadership as people from other generations."

Gen Z Student, Age 20 - Stevens Institute of Technology

Generations share some similarities and have many differences. Growing up under different circumstances, world environments, and parenting styles affect their behaviors and outlook on life. Politics, technology, and the shifting work environment all play a role in how Gen Z will fit into the modern workforce.

Some of the biggest reasons for the differences between Gen Z and previous generations is their early exposure to modern technology. There is a reason Gen Z is sometimes referred to as iGen. Most people in Gen Z grew up with smartphone technology and social media. They are by far more technologically savvy than previous generations. This gives them valuable knowledge heading into the workforce. They certainly have an advantage when it comes to understanding technology that is transforming the workforce. That knowledge will come in handy for becoming the future leaders of organizations.

Another environmental factor that Gen Z faced while being raised is economics. Growing up, Millennials lived under a strong economy, whereas all of Gen Z still lived with their parents during the 2008 recession. This difference lead to most Millennials being raised under good economic times, whereas Gen Z was generally raised to be more frugal. They have been conditioned to be more responsible with their finances because that was how they were raised. This translates to spending habits, personal finance, as well as understanding economics in a business setting. The ability to be financially responsible affects salary negotiation and expectations. Companies may need to offer higher compensation packages to incoming Gen Z employees. Additionally, this financial frugality gives them an advantage in being responsible with company finances as well, which would be a huge asset to companies as Gen Z heads into leadership roles.

Another key difference between Millennials and Gen Z is how they view collaboration and independence. A big attribute of Millennials is their desire for teamwork and collaboration in work spaces. Many companies shifted to meet this demand by forming more teams and breaking down cubicle walls to form more collaborative environments. Gen Z is still capable of teamwork and collaboration, because that is what is expected when moving into corporate America, however they are a much more independent generation. They still enjoy collaboration more than generations before Millennials, but many people in Gen Z enjoy their independence and are comfortable being delegated tasks they can complete on their own. They thrive on competition. A disadvantage here would be that companies have recently adjusted to Millennials to develop that collaborative work structure, so adjusting to Gen Z could mean another organizational shift. An advantage, however, would be the ability to rely on individual employees to accomplish tasks without needing too much collaboration and teamwork, which involves more communication and the potential for communication breakdown. Additionally, leaders often need to be relied on independently as well as able to work with the team they lead, which are skills Gen Z has.

As the workforce becomes more diverse, it only makes sense that having a generation of more diverse leaders will lead to a more open work environment and better equality in opportunities.

Gen Z is going to be the next crop of leaders in the workforce sooner than we think. They will be more technologically savvy than previous generations and will transform the work environment as we know it. Their independence and teamwork skills will allow them to lead all types of work environments. Their diversity allows them to lead people from diverse backgrounds and interests, fostering a more productive and enjoyable work environment. Although they are not as experienced as leaders in corporate America just yet, they certainly bring some advantages to leadership in the workforce.

After describing what is leadership potential and listing the qualities of a good leader, we described the pros and cons of Gen Z and whether the group has a high leadership potential. As a conclusion of our research, we believe that Gen Z has a huge potential compared to previous generations, and needs to capitalize on it.

CHAPTER REFERENCES

Bridgespan Group (n.d.) "What Leadership Potential Really Means." Retrieved May 7, 2019 from: www.bridgespan.org/getdoc/edd4e6a9-93de-478a-a018-62ee7fc3ac90/what-leadership-potential-really-means.

Mccarthy, D. (2018). Assessing Leadership Potential Using the 9 Box Model." Retrieved May 6, 2019 from: www.thebalancecareers.com/9-box-matrix-2276064.

GEN Z CO-AUTHORS

GORAV KUMAR
Gorav is senior Quantitative Finance student at Stevens Institute of Technology. He is also pursuing a masters in Business Intelligence and Analytics as part of the college's 4+1 program. He will be joining DBRS full time in May as a Quantitative Analyst.

ELOI PRADIER
Eloi is a freshman Finance student at Stevens Institute of Technology. International Student and had many experiences with different type of leaders through different cultures.

JESSE PRIEST
Jesse is a junior Business and Technology student at Stevens Institute of Technology. With work experience in engineering, digital marketing, consulting, maintenance, merchandising, and real estate development, he has been a part of various different work environments and worked with many different types of leaders.

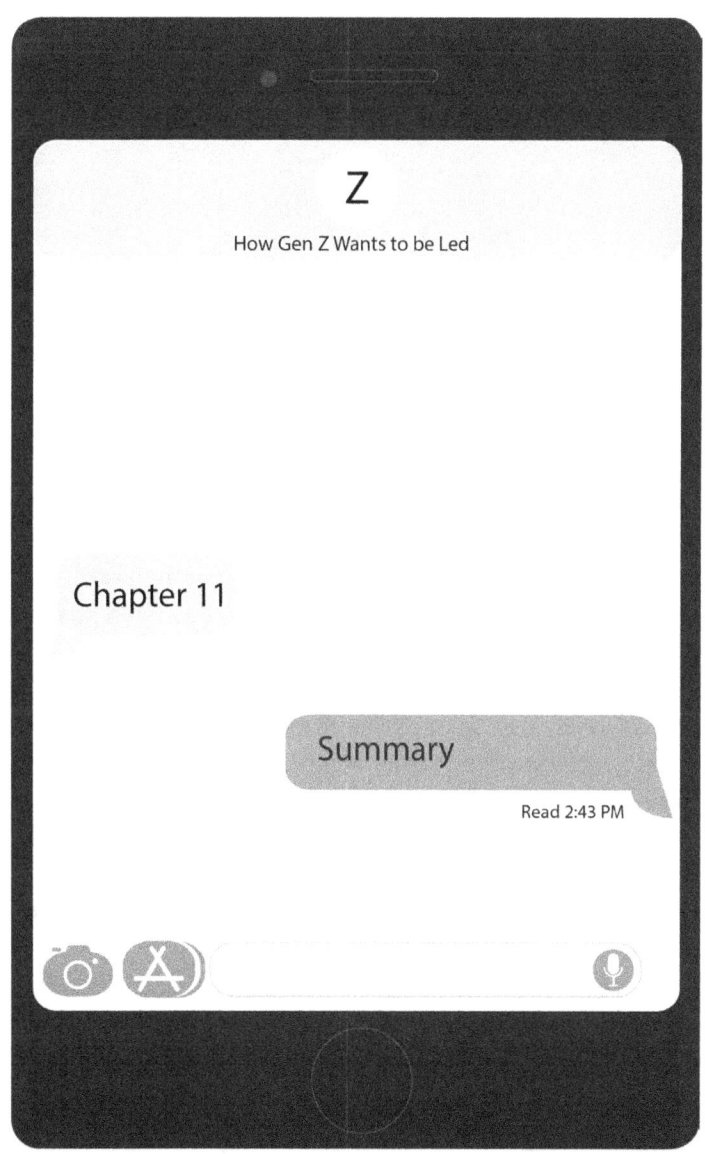

Z

How Gen Z Wants to be Led

Chapter 11

Summary

Read 2:43 PM

"Real leaders are happy to zig while others zag. They understand that in an era of hyper-competition and non-stop disruption, the only way to stand out from the crowd is to stand for something special."

Bill Taylor

As members of Gen Z transition from academia to industry, organizations are tasked with incorporating five drastically different generations into one cohesive workforce. The traditionalists and baby boomers, who have always valued expertise and loyalty, were first introduced to the entrepreneurial culture of Generation X. Though Generation X was slightly more tech savvy and much more independent, it was not until the Millennials introduced unconventional work hours and far deeper technological integrations that the degree to which each generation is different from the one before it was truly illuminated. The multigenerational workforce has been adapting for years, but what about Gen Z is so special?

Gen Z has only just begun to disrupt the labor market. Having grown up in an age of pervasive technology, Gen Z is inherently forward-thinking and mature. With an unparalleled ability to blend Artificial Intelligence with Human Intelligence, Gen Z can easily leverage rare technological skills while bringing other practical skills to the workforce. With plenty of professional experience prior to entering the workforce, Gen Z is fully prepared to not only be responsible for their careers, but also to contribute serious value to companies as soon as they are introduced.

Gen Z values challenging, meaningful work. If a member of Gen Z's skills are not being fully utilized, they will most likely feel dissatisfied with their work. They always want to learn and thrive in positions where they can multitask and showcase all of their skills. With a plethora of skills and a dedication to doing meaningful work, Gen Z also values a work life balance. Companies are beginning to adjust to flexible work hours in order to accommodate this demand. Furthermore, as Gen Z seeks a more dynamic workday, cooperative and online workspaces should thrive.

As members of Gen Z move into leadership positions, they prepare to implement their values on a wider scale and transform the workforce for future success. They seek diversity and creativity, and will expect both of their employees. New ideas are valued, and outside-the-box thinking is considered the norm. Gen Z wants to stand out from their competitors but still stay true to their values, impacting their decisions for corporate strategy and regular workday tasks. As leaders, they will look for new ways to do business, differentiating themselves through their driven attitudes and unique way of thinking.

Possibility the greatest benefit of the entry of Gen Z in the workforce is their ability to embrace change. They have grown up in an era of extraordinary technological advancement and cultural evolution, and are therefore able to easily adapt to fast-paced change. As employees, they are always willing to learn, seeking out new skills and more efficient ways to complete tasks. They are born innovators and constantly looking for ways to improve themselves and their teams.

When you translate Gen Z's traits into leadership styles, it appears that Gen Z might prefer a culture that enables change and the need to lead toward a technology driven atmosphere, automating processes and utilizing technology in every aspect of the business to optimize results. They also may prefer to work independently, not reliant of traditional office hierarchy. They may prefer to seek their own resources and encourage employees to seek out information immediately, rather than wait for a conference call or meeting next Tuesday (Blazek, 2016).

In this book, Gen Zers have shared their own views on their potential to disrupt the workforce. These thoughts on leadership, ranging from communications to technological change, come straight from the mouths of Gen Z themselves. As more members of Gen Z begin their careers, it is imperative for the work-force to be prepared. Not only do they seek dynamic jobs with value-focused companies, but they are willing to enact the necessary change in their organizations.

RELATE, CREATE AND RELEASE

Madden (2018) captured three key attributes that Gen Z wants in its leaders; **Relate, Create and Release:**

RELATE

For an immensely social generation, relationships are of the highest importance for Gen Z, and are viewed as being central to effective leadership. The function of leadership is deeply founded in relationships, being marked by vision, courage, and the capacity to inspire others to follow.

Gen Z are looking for leaders who are real, authentic, relational and genuine. They are quickly disenchanted by leaders they perceive to be fake, superior, or out-of-reach. They crave an authentic connection with their leaders, rather than a distant, removed authority figure who takes no interest in them and does not 'speak their language'.

CREATE

GeZ are looking for leaders who actively create an engaging culture. Culture is the environment and lived reality that is created in an organization; it fills the gap between what is announced and what is actually experienced.

A culture which will facilitate greater engagement from Gen Z is one where they feel safe to be known, contribute and learn. A leader who will effectively engage Gen Z will build on listening and facilitate a culture where people are encouraged to contribute ideas and solutions, rather than having their ideas shut down or be limited to simply completing tasks. When building multigenerational teams and leading Gen Z, leaders who listen to the input of others will not only be more informed but will gain the trust and respect of team members. This approach will bring out the best of each team member and often open a door for reciprocal interactions, as people are much more likely to listen to leaders who have listened to the followers.

RELEASE

Gen Z are looking for leaders to set an example with their lives worth emulating, who have a focus on empowering and releasing others to fulfil their potential. Leaders can motivate and inspire Gen Zs by communicating high expectations to their followers and inspiring them to be committed and part of the shared vision of the organization, through their own example.

Empowering and transformative leaders understand that the greatest asset in their organization is the people. That the greatest potential, ideas, innovations and possibilities reside in the minds and hearts of those in their team.

Whilst Gen Z have been told repeatedly that they abound with potential, and have a desire for self-actualization and to make a difference, it is not possible for this to be discovered and achieved on their own. Transformational leadership that is empowering requires perceptive, committed, older leaders to identify the specific gifts, talents, skills and interests of their Gen Z team members, invest in them, build on their strengths, identify any untapped potential, and instill in them a confidence to go beyond their comfort zones.

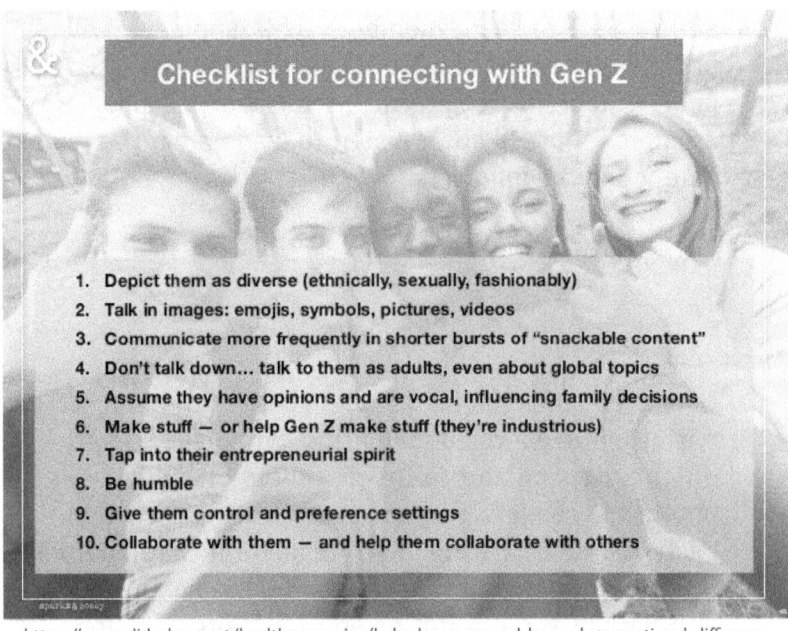

Checklist for connecting with Gen Z

1. Depict them as diverse (ethnically, sexually, fashionably)
2. Talk in images: emojis, symbols, pictures, videos
3. Communicate more frequently in shorter bursts of "snackable content"
4. Don't talk down... talk to them as adults, even about global topics
5. Assume they have opinions and are vocal, influencing family decisions
6. Make stuff — or help Gen Z make stuff (they're industrious)
7. Tap into their entrepreneurial spirit
8. Be humble
9. Give them control and preference settings
10. Collaborate with them — and help them collaborate with others

https://www.slideshare.net/healthcareseries/baby-boomers-and-beyond-generational-differences-and-quality-challengesjanet-hahn-western-michigan-university

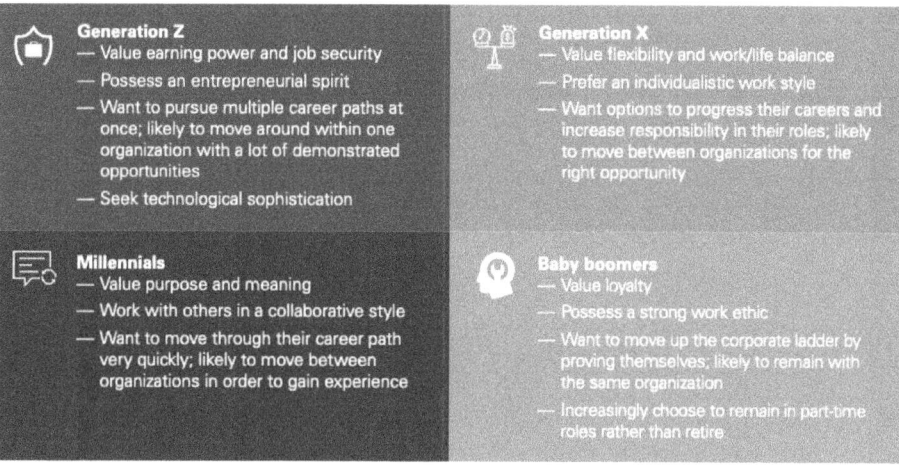

https://advisory.kpmg.us/content/dam/advisory/en/pdfs/generation-z-talent.pdf

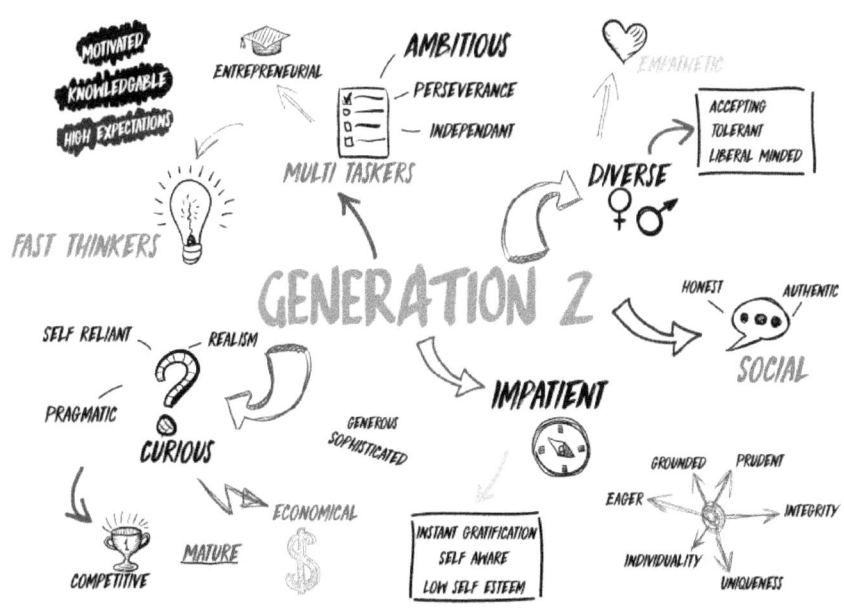

http://dcp-uk.co.uk/generation-z-every-brand-needs-know/generation-z/

CHAPTER REFERENCES

Blazek, K. (2016). The Leadership Style of Gen Z. Retrieved May 5, 2019 from https://www.truscore.com/360-feedback-resources/gen-z/

Madden, C. (2018). Gen Z: Three Leadership Foundations. Retrieved May 4, 2019 from: https://www.linkedin.com/pulse/gen-z-three-leadership-foundations-claire-madden/

ABOUT THE AUTHORS

Dr. Richard Dool

Dr. Richard Dool is currently the Managing Director of LeaderocityTM, LLC, a management consultancy offering solutions for change management, strategic development, leadership communication and organizational renewal.
Dr. Dool is on the faculty at the School of Communication and Information at Rutgers University, where he is also the Director of the Masters in Communication and Media program.

He has a MA in Strategic Communication and Leadership, a MS in Management and a Doctorate in Management/Organizational Processes. Dr. Dool is an active researcher and presenter in these areas and has published on the concepts of Change FatigueTM and LeaderocityTM. He is the author of "Enervative Change: The Impact of Persistent Change Initiatives on Job Satisfaction.

He has a comprehensive and diverse executive level leadership background including leading an $800M division of AT&T, global executive leadership roles (GE), and serving 12 years as CEO of both public and private companies. Background includes rescuing a company from near bankruptcy, leading the acquisition or divestiture of 11 companies and effectively managing companies in the US, UK, China, Brazil, Germany, France, India and Australia. He has been on the Board of Directors of five different companies as well as a member of several Boards of Advisors.
www.linkedin.com/in/richard-dool

OUR OTHER GEN Z CO-AUTHORS

DaniAnn Costagliola - is currently a sophomore at Stevens Institute of Technology and she is majoring in Business and Technology with concentrations in Management and Information Systems. DaniAnn is a member of generation Z and is looking forward to the future and entering the ever-changing workplace. She believes this is a valuable learning experience that will help her in her journey in finding employment in the field of management.

Julia Dwight - is a freshman Business and Technology Major at Stevens Institute of Technology. Outside of class, she serves as the Co-Chair of Festivities for the Entertainment Committee, and event planning group on campus. She believes that Generation Z will be able to revolutionize the workforce, ushering in increased diversity and technological advancement in business.

Julianne Greco - a junior at Stevens Institute of Technology working toward her Bachelor's Degree in Quantitative Finance. When she's not in the classroom she is at her internship in New York City helping marketers streamline their digital content generation. As a member of Generation Z who is already in the workforce, Julianne thinks this research is pivotal as Generation Z begins to disrupt the workforce.

Meghan Hom - Meghan is currently a sophomore at Stevens Institute of Technology and she is majoring in Quantitative Finance with a concentration and minor in Computer Science. Meghan is a part of Generation Z and is eager to see how this book will impact Gen Z and the workforce. She believes that it will inspire current and future generations in the workforce.

Gregory Kane - Gregory aims to major in both marketing and the Visual Arts at Stevens Institute of Technology. When he isn't found drawing or adding trope-filled sentences to his bio, he can be found experimenting in multiple fields, including music and game design. Gregory is a member of Generation Z who believes the group has much to offer in the coming years and has aimed to reflect that in the front and back covers which he designed.

Melissa Kosar - is a freshman at Stevens Institute of Technology, studying to earn a Bachelor's Degree in Business and Technology with concentrations in Marketing and Visual Arts & Technology, and minoring in International Business. Outside of class, she serves as the Editor-in-Chief of Stevens' Fashion Association of Marketing & Entrepreneurship magazine. As a member of Generation Z, Melissa believes that this research is extremely vital for all members of the workforce in order to expect fluidity and cooperation amongst workers in the coming future. She feels that with Gen Z entering the workforce will bring a major shift in the culture across many industries and without research like this we would not be prepared.

Emma Murphy - Emma is currently a senior at Stevens Institute of Technology and she is majoring in Business and Technology with concentrations in Marketing and Music and Technology. Emma is one of the oldest members of Generation Z being born in 1996. She is excited to represent the older side of the generation. She feels this research is important to document as the workforce does not currently cover her needs.

Daniel Pennell - Daniel is currently a freshman at Stevens Institute of Technology. He is majoring in Economics and minoring in International Business. Daniel is a member of Generation Z and is intrigued on how his fellow members view the future of the work force when compared to how the previous generations felt when in the same position. He believes that this newly acquired insight can help prepare the work force for the changes that will be implemented over the next decade along with help him be a catalyst for that change.

Sara Persau - is a freshman at Stevens Institute of Technology, studying toward a Bachelor's Degree in Finance. As a member of Generation Z, Sara believes this research will facilitate improvement in the workforce and is excited to contribute to the documentation of her generation, whose future is led by Gen Z. By viewing the future from the perspective of Gen Z, Sara is confident that they will be able to transform the workplace and bring about effective change. She hopes that this vital research will lead her in pursuing a future in a revolutionized world of business.

Sergio Scardigno - Sergio is currently a sophomore at Stevens Institute of Technology. He is majoring in Music Technology and minoring in Marketing. Sergio is part of Gen Z himself, and finds it encouraging that other generations are willing to hear Gen Z out on how they would work best as professionals. He believes this book will help to inspire a cohesive, successful, inter-generational workforce in the future.

SUMMARY

www.ingramcontent.com/pod-product-compliance
Lightning Source LLC
Chambersburg PA
CBHW072138170526
45158CB00004BA/1421